# FRE

## Just for Business

### Jane Millar and Marilyn Farr

## Study Guide

### Oxford University Press

Oxford University Press  Walton Street  Oxford OX2 6DP

*Oxford  New York  Toronto*
*Delhi  Bombay  Calcutta  Madras  Karachi*
*Petaling Jaya  Singapore  Hong Kong  Tokyo*
*Nairobi  Dar es Salaam  Cape Town*
*Melbourne  Auckland*

and associated companies in

*Berlin  Ibadan*

*Oxford* is a trade mark of Oxford University Press

ISBN  0  19  912143 5

Illustrations by Patricia Moffett, Joan Corlass and Gecko Limited

**Acknowledgements**

The authors wish to acknowledge the help of Jean Burrell, Matthew Hunter, June Jones, Mike Parsons and Danielle Teper for their contributions to the research that went into this publication. They also wish to thank Yvonne de Henseler for her support and encouragement, and Janet Caldwell for her help in preparing the tapescript.

Printed and bound in Great Britain by
Butler & Tanner Ltd, Frome and London

# Contents

# About the course

Welcome to **French *Just for Business*,** a short, practical language course for the hard-pressed business learner. This course will not turn you into a fluent French speaker overnight but it will equip you with some basic communication skills in French, and above all it will demonstrate that you are making the effort to learn the language of the country you want to do business in! It is suitable for both near beginners and those with rusty school French, who need a revision course with a business emphasis.

You can do most of your learning from the cassettes alone. This is because one of the aims of the course is to train you to understand spoken French on the telephone, in meetings and in other situations where you are not able to refer to the printed word. We therefore recommend that you listen to each Unit at least once before you refer to any of the printed material, apart from the Pen and Paper Exercises, in the Study Guide.

You'll hear a series of conversations in French, as you follow the progress of representatives of two British companies selling their products in France. English narrators guide you through step by step, explaining the language you hear and inviting you to join in the dialogues. The accompanying Study Guide contains much useful back-up information, and we strongly recommend that you use it regularly to consolidate your learning.

To get the most out of your course we recommend that you tackle it in the following way:

1 Do your initial learning of each Unit somewhere where you can really concentrate. Car journeys, though ideal for reinforcement, are not really suitable for the learning of new material.

2 Listen to the cassette as often as you can, every day if possible. 'Little and often' is the key to successful language learning. Don't expect to master a Unit by listening to it once only. You will need to listen to it several times and to replay difficult sections as often as necessary. Use pause and replay buttons if you have them and remember to make a note of the number on your tape counter as you begin a new Unit.

3 Read through the notes provided in the Study Guide after listening to each Unit. These notes are intended to provide you with a summary of the new language contained in each Unit and with visual reinforcement of what you have learned from the cassettes.

The notes on each Unit have five Sections:

## 1 Language for you to use

This is the language you will need to produce yourself and therefore you should concentrate on learning and practising the language in this Section. Do not go on to the next Unit until you feel you have mastered these words and expressions. Try to get someone else to test you once you have learned them thoroughly.

## 2 Language for you to recognize

The language in this Section is what you have heard other people use on the cassette and what you must therefore learn to recognize. Although at this stage you only need a 'passive' knowledge of this language, it is important not to neglect this section as you need to understand in order to respond effectively. You may also want to 'activate' this language later on, if, for example, you are receiving instead of making a telephone call. If you already know some French, you may, of course, feel able to do this from the start.

## 3 Pen and Paper Exercises

Every now and then, if you are listening to the cassettes, you will come across the mention of a Pen and Paper Exercise. These are optional exercises which will improve your listening skills. They do not require you to write anything in French; in fact, all you usually need to do is tick a box or draw a line as you listen to the relevant part of your cassette again. Do these exercises the first time you listen to the tape if you feel ready, but some are more difficult and you may need to come back to them later.

## 4 Language maps

These are a summary in diagrammatic or illustrated form of the dialogues you have heard on the cassettes complete with possible variations. They will help you make up and practise your own dialogues.

## 5 Language debrief

As well as a brief Language Reference Section at the back, we also guide you through some basic points about the structure of the language as they come up in each Unit.

At the end of the Guide you will find a Language Reference Section, a Vocabulary Section, the answers to the Pen and Paper Exercises and some useful tips about doing business in France. We also suggest how you can develop your French once you have completed this course.

Your pack also contains some prompt cards with key phrases for you to remember. You can slip them into your diary and use them for instant recall, when you are conversing in French.

# Unit 1 *Making contact by telephone*

***Checklist***   By the end of this Unit you should be able to:

❏  get through to the right person

❏  deal with some difficulties

❏  understand when to call back.

But you'll have to wait till the next Unit to learn how
to leave a message yourself!

**Key words and phrases**
*for you to use*

## Greetings and introductions

| Bonjour | madame | *Good morning/afternoon* |
|---|---|---|
| Au revoir | mademoiselle monsieur | *Goodbye* |

C'est ...... de la société ......
à ...... , en Angleterre

*My name is ...... from ......*
*Ltd, in ......, England*

## Getting through to the right person

Je voudrais parler à
Monsieur ......

*I'd like to speak to Mr ......*

Est-ce que je peux parler à
Madame/Mademoiselle ......

*May I speak to Mrs/Miss ......*

## Getting through to the right department

Le service marketing, s'il vous
plaît

*Marketing Department*
*please*

| | | | |
|---|---|---|---|
| | technique | *Technical Services* | |
| | de production | *Production* | |
| | du personnel | *Personnel* | |
| Le service | de la comptabilité | *Accounts* | *Department* |
| | des achats | *Purchasing* | |
| | des ventes | *Sales* | |
| | après-vente | *After-sales* | |
| | import/export | *Import/Export* | |

8

## Saying when you'll call back

| | |
|---|---|
| Non merci, je rappellerai ...... | *No thank you, I'll call back ......* |
| plus tard | *later* |
| cette après-midi | *this afternoon* |
| demain (matin/après-midi) | *tomorrow (am/pm)* |
| la semaine prochaine | *next week* |
| lundi | *Monday* |
| mardi | *Tuesday* |
| mercredi | *Wednesday* |
| jeudi | *Thursday* |
| vendredi | *Friday* |
| (Quand) est-ce que je peux le/la joindre/rappeler? | *(When) can I call him/her (back)?* |

## Other useful phrases

| | |
|---|---|
| Bonjour, monsieur. Vous parlez anglais? | *Good morning. Do you speak English?* |
| Bien sûr! | *Of course!* |
| Pardon, madame/monsieur, je ne comprends pas | *I'm sorry, I don't understand* |
| Voulez-vous répéter cela (plus lentement)? | *Can you repeat that (more slowly)?* |

**Key words and phrases**
*for you to recognize*

## Greetings you will hear

| | |
|---|---|
| Bonjour, société ...... à votre service | *Good morning, ...... Ltd, can I help you?* |

## Putting you through

| | |
|---|---|
| Allô. Ici la société ...... | *Hello, ...... Ltd* |
| De la part de qui? | *Who's speaking?* |
| Ne quittez pas | *Hold the line* |
| La ligne est occupée | *The line's engaged* |
| Il/Elle est en communication | *He/She is on the line* |
| Voulez-vous patienter? | *Would you like to hold?* |
| Je vous le/la passe | *Putting you through* |
| Vous êtes en ligne | *You're through* |
| Ici le bureau de Monsieur/Madame ...... | *Mr/Mrs ......'s office* |
| Monsieur/Madame ...... à l'appareil | *Mr/Mrs ...... on the line* |

## Sorry, I didn't catch that

| | |
|---|---|
| Voulez-vous répéter/épeler votre nom? | *Can you repeat/spell your name?* |
| Comment ça s'écrit? | *How do you spell that?* |

## Understanding why they're not there

| | |
|---|---|
| Je suis désolé(e) ⎤ | *I'm sorry* |
| Je regrette ⎦ | |
| Monsieur/Madame ...... est absent(e) pour l'instant | *Mr/Mrs ...... isn't here at the moment* |
| Mademoiselle ...... n'est pas là aujourd'hui | *Miss ...... isn't here today* |
| Il/Elle est ...... | *He/She's ......* |
|    en réunion/conférence | *in a meeting* |
|    en déplacement | *away* |
|    en voyage d'affaires | *away on business* |
|    en vacances | *on holiday* |
|    malade | *ill* |
|    pris(e) | *busy* |

## And when you can call back

| | |
|---|---|
| Vous pouvez rappeler ...... | *You can call back ......* |
|    vers deux heures | *around 2 o'clock* |
|    demain matin | *tomorrow morning* |
|    avant onze heures | *before 11 o'clock* |

## Section 3  *Pen and paper exercises*

**The answers to all Pen and Paper Exercises can be found in the Section beginning on p 77.**

1 Listen to the tape and match the people to the departments in which they work.

    1 Technical Services        a M. Martin
    2 After-sales Service        b M. Paget
    3 Marketing                c Mlle Dupuis
    4 Accounts                 d Mme Roche

2 Write down the names of people and places as the caller spells them for you.

    1 _____
    2 _____

3 The pictures below show the *real* reasons why the person you are calling can't speak to you. Listen to the tape and tick the appropriate box to indicate whether the reason you hear is true or false.

☐ *True*    ☐ *False*        ☐ *True*    ☐ *False*

☐ *True*    ☐ *False*        ☐ *True*    ☐ *False*

4 Listen to Mme Dubois and enter in your diary below, the one time when you and M. Dupuis are both free to talk to each other on the phone.

Sunday

Monday TODAY 11-12 Meeting with John Roberts, SCI TECH LTD

Tuesday

Wednesday ALL-DAY SALES CONFERENCE
Dep. 7.30 a.m.
Home by 9pm?

Thursday 4.30pm. Dep. Heathrow – for Düsseldorf

Friday TRADE FAIR – DÜSSELDORF
plane leaves 6.30p.m.

Saturday

**Language debrief**

## Saying what you would like to do

Je voudrais ......                     *I'd like to ......*

To this phrase you can add the basic form of any verb (a word denoting an action) in order to say what you would like to do, e.g.

Je voudrais | parler à ......          *I'd like to* | *speak to ......*
            | rappeler                              | *call back*

## Inviting someone to do something

Voulez-vous ......?                    *Would you like to ......?*

Just as in the examples above, you can add verbs to this phrase if you want to invite someone to do something, e.g.

Voulez-vous parler à                   *Would you like to speak to*
M. Martin?                             *M. Martin?*

Voulez-vous épeler votre nom? *Could you spell your name?*
Voulez-vous rappeler?                  *Would you like to call back?*

## Names of departments

Many of the names of departments of a company are expressed as: *the department of ......,* **le service de ......,** followed by the name of the function. You will meet **de, du, de la** and **des** used to express *of* in this context.

In other cases you just add the word for the function after **le service,** e.g. **le service marketing.**

The choice of form is a matter of common usage, rather than a set of rules to follow. At this stage learn these titles as set phrases. The grammar will be explained later.

## Asking questions

### Questions which require the answer 'yes' or 'no'

There are three common ways of asking this type of question in French:

1   By letting your voice go up at the end of the sentence, e.g.

    Vous parlez anglais?          *Do you speak English?*

2   By  changing the word order, e.g.

    Parlez-vous anglais?          *Do you speak English?*

3   By putting **est-ce que** (which means nothing in itself, but merely indicates that a question is being asked) at the beginning, e.g.

    Est-ce que vous parlez        *Do you speak English?*
    anglais?

### Questions beginning with a question word

By this we mean questions beginning with words like *when, where, how, how much, why,* etc. Again there are various possibilities. One is simply to place the question word before **est-ce que ......**, as in the question:

**Quand** est-ce que je peux     **When** *can I get hold of*
le joindre?                      *him?*

(Note that the **d** of **quand** is pronounced as if it were **t**. See notes on liaison in the Language Reference Section.)

We'll discuss other question forms as we meet them.

# Language map

Bonjour, Leroy et Fils.

**Bonjour, madame .
Je voudrais parler à
Monsieur Leroy, s'il
vous plaît.**

De la part de qui?

**C'est Les Wilcox
de la société Fenestral
à Thame, Angleterre.**

Ne quittez pas.

Je vous le passe.

Bonjour. Leroy à
l'appareil.

**Bonjour, monsieur.
Parlez-vous anglais?**

Oui, bien sûr.          Non, pas du tout.

Monsieur Leroy est
en communication.
Voulez-vous patienter?

**Oui, bien sûr.**          **Non, merci.
Je rappellerai.**

Vous êtes en ligne.

Allô. Ici le bureau de
Monsieur Leroy.
Mademoiselle Prunier à
l'appareil.

**Bonjour, madame.
Est-ce que je peux
parler à Monsieur
Leroy?**

C'est de la part de qui?

**De Les Wilcox de la
société Fenestral.**

Voulez-vous répéter
votre nom?

**C'est Wilcox.**

Merci. Je vous le passe.

Bonjour. Leroy à l'appareil.

Je suis désolée.
Monsieur Leroy est
absent pour l'instant.

**Quand est-ce que je
peux le joindre?**

Cette après-midi
peut-être?

**Merci bien, madame.
Je rappellerai cette
après-midi.**

# Unit 2 *More about telephoning*

**Checklist**

By the end of this Unit you should be able to:

❏ deal confidently with telephone numbers

❏ leave basic details about yourself including what you are phoning about and

❏ ask for someone to ring you back.

You will also be able to make, change and cancel appointments.

**Key words and phrases**
*for you to use*

## Leaving basic details about who you are

| | |
|---|---|
| Le nom de ma société est ...... | *The name of my company is ......* |
| L'adresse de ma société est ...... | *The address of my company is ....* |
| Le numéro de téléphone est ...... | *The telephone number is ......* |
| L'indicatif est ...... | *The code is ......* |

## Saying what you are telephoning for

| | |
|---|---|
| C'est au sujet de ...... | *It's about ......* |
| votre lettre | *your letter* |
| notre contrat | *our contract* |
| notre facture | *our invoice* |
| votre visite chez nous | *your visit to us* |

## Leaving a message for someone to ring you back

| | |
|---|---|
| Il/Elle peut me rappeler ...... | *Can he/she ring me back......* |
| avant onze heures et demie? | *before 11.30?* |
| dans quinze minutes? | *in 15 minutes?* |
| C'est urgent | *It's urgent* |

# Talking about appointments

### Requesting an appointment

Je voudrais prendre
rendez-vous avec ......

*I'd like to make an
appointment with ......*

### Fixing a date

La première semaine
de septembre, si possible

*The first week in
September, if possible*

Je suis libre le mercredi
ou le jeudi

*I'm free Wednesday
or Thursday*

### Changing a date

Pourriez-vous changer/
avancer/remettre la date du
rendez-vous/de la réunion?

*Could you change/bring
forward/postpone the date
of the appointment/meeting?*

### Confirming and cancelling appointments

Je voudrais confirmer/
annuler notre rendez-vous
du 15 février

*I'd like to confirm/
cancel our appointment
of 15th February*

# Key words and phrases
## for you to recognize

## Understanding requests for basic information

| | |
|---|---|
| Quel est votre nom? | *What is your name?* |
| Quel est le nom de votre société? | *What is your company's name?* |
| Quelle est l'adresse? | *What is the address?* |
| Quel est votre numéro de téléphone? | *What is your telephone number?* |
| Quel est l'indicatif? | *What is the area code?* |
| C'est quel poste? | *What is your extension?* |
| C'est à quel sujet? | *What is it about?* |

## Understanding questions about messages

| | |
|---|---|
| Voulez-vous laisser un message? | *Do you want to leave a message?* |
| Avez-vous un message à lui transmettre? | |
| C'est entendu | *It (the message) is understood* |

## Understanding offers of assistance

| | |
|---|---|
| Est-ce que je peux vous être utile? | *Can I help you?* |

## Understanding questions about appointments

| | |
|---|---|
| Quelle date vous convient? | *What date suits you?* |
| Quel jour de préférence? | *What day do you prefer?* |
| Je vais chercher son agenda | *I'll just get his/her diary* |
| Est-ce que quatorze heures vous convient? | *Does 2 pm suit you?* |

## Other useful phrases

| | |
|---|---|
| Il est quelle heure en Angleterre/en France? | *What time is it in England/in France?* |
| Est-ce que vous avez le bon numéro? | *Do you have the right number?* |

**Pen and paper exercises**

1    If the telephone number you hear does not match the one given below, write the correct version in the space provided.

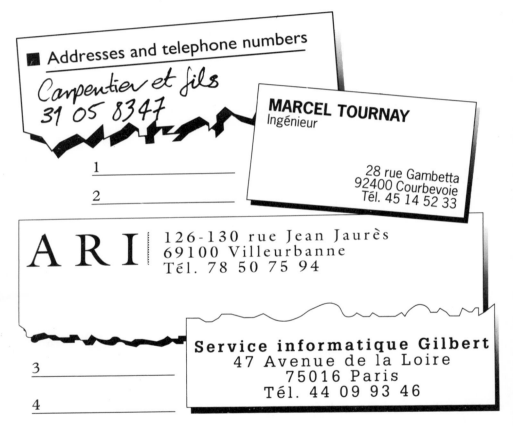

■ Addresses and telephone numbers

*Carpentier et fils*
*31 05 8347*

1 _____

2 _____

**MARCEL TOURNAY**
Ingénieur

28 rue Gambetta
92400 Courbevoie
Tél. 45 14 52 33

A R I    126-130 rue Jean Jaurès
69100 Villeurbanne
Tél. 78 50 75 94

**Service informatique Gilbert**
47 Avenue de la Loire
75016 Paris
Tél. 44 09 93 46

3 _____

4 _____

2    Say the following telephone and fax numbers aloud after you hear the question on the tape. Then listen to the correct version.

1.   54 45 08 11        2.   72 89 03 19
3.   94 15 31 33        4.   53 67 18 77

**3** Listen to the three conversations on tape and draw a line to link the message number firstly with the person or department it is for and then with the subject of the message. Take care! We've listed more people and messages than you actually hear!

| *Message 1* | for | a) | the Director's secretary | about | i) | a letter |
|---|---|---|---|---|---|---|
| *Message 2* | | b) | the Managing Director | | ii) | a bill |
| *Message 3* | | c) | Accounts | | iii) | a visit |
| | | d) | Sales | | iv) | a contract |

**4** Listen to the answerphone messages and complete or amend the notes as necessary.

1 M. Carrière from Logeay called. He wants Mrs Phillips to ring him. I'm not sure what it's about, I'm afraid.

2 Urgent message from Mlle Prunier of Labègue for Mrs Cartwright, about something being cancelled. (Sorry, couldn't understand the rest!)

3 M. Leroy from Giroud rang to confirm he'll be arriving at Heathrow on Thursday at 3 pm on flight BA264.

**5** Number the recorded messages in the order in which you hear them.

*Number*

The number you have dialled is no longer in use. We regret that we are unable to connect your call. ☐

This number is not currently in use. ☐

Please note that this number has changed. Please dial 54 66 87 05. ☐

All the lines for the Bordeaux area are in use. Please try again later. ☐

_Section 4_ **Language debrief**

## Masculine and feminine

In French not just people, but all words denoting living beings, inanimate objects and concepts (nouns, grammatically speaking) have a gender, either masculine or feminine.

Other words which accompany nouns, such as the words for _the_ and _a(n)_, or which replace them, such as _it_ or _they_, must also take the appropriate masculine or feminine form; in grammatical terms, they must 'agree'.

Unfortunately there is no obvious logic to help you remember the gender of words. You simply have to learn them as you go along. But don't worry about making mistakes in gender; you'll normally be understood even if you do.

## 'The' and 'a'

| | |
|---|---|
| **le** monsieur | _the_ gentleman |
| **un** monsieur | _a_ gentleman |
| **la** dame | _the_ lady |
| **une** dame | _a_ lady |

but this word is also masculine:

| | |
|---|---|
| **le** rendez-vous | _the_ appointment |
| **un** rendez-vous | _an_ appointment |

whereas the word for _meeting_ is feminine:

| | |
|---|---|
| **la** réunion | _the_ meeting |
| **une** réunion | _a_ meeting |

You'll be pleased to hear that the plural form for _the_ is **les** for both genders.

Note: **le** and **la** also mean _him_ and _her_, as in:

| | |
|---|---|
| Quand est-ce que je peux **le/la** rappeler? | _When can I call **him/her** back?_ |

24

## 'Of the' (du, de la, des)

These forms all mean *of the.* The masculine **du** can be regarded as a contracted form of **de + le,** and plural **des** as a contraction of **de + les.**

| | |
|---|---|
| La date **du** rendez-vous | *The date **of the** appointment* |
| **de la** réunion | ***of the** meeting* |
| **des** conférences | ***of the** meetings* |

## Asking 'which' and 'what'

To ask *which* or *what* use **quel**, e.g.

| | |
|---|---|
| **Quel** est **le** nom de votre société? | ***What*** *is the name of your company?* |
| **Quelle** est **la** date de la réunion? | ***What*** *is the date of the meeting?* |

In later units we'll meet:

| | |
|---|---|
| **Quels/Quelles** sont ...... ? | ***What/Which*** *are ......?* |

Don't worry about the various forms for masculine, feminine, singular and plural. They are all pronounced in the same way.

## 'Your' and 'our'

In the case of words meaning *your* and *our* there are different forms for singular and plural only.

| | |
|---|---|
| **votre** nom | ***your*** *name* |
| **vos** noms | ***your*** *names* |
| **votre** adresse | ***your*** *address* |
| **vos** factures | ***your*** *invoices* |
| **notre** numéro | ***our*** *number* |
| **nos** contrats | ***our*** *contracts* |
| **notre** visite | ***our*** *visit* |
| **nos** lettres | ***our*** *letters* |

## Saying what it's about

**C'est** = *it is ...... (it's ...... ),* or in a question *is it?*

**C'est** au sujet de notre visite    ***It's*** *about our visit*

| **C'est** à quel sujet? | *What **is it** about?* |

Note that we say: **au sujet de** - *about,* or literally *on the subject of,* but: **à quel sujet** means literally *on what subject.*

## *Your place or mine?*

| Votre visite **chez nous** | *Your visit **to us*** |
| Il est **chez nous** | *He's **at our place / with us*** |

**Chez nous** is a useful little phrase whose precise meaning depends on the context. As you can see from the above examples, it can mean *to us, to our place* or *at our place,* where *place* can refer to one's home or company. If you're making international comparisons it can even mean *in our country.*

## *Asking whether it's possible*

These are some more phrases to which you can add another verb, this time in order to ask if something is possible. They are all related in meaning, and come from the same verb, **pouvoir** (*to be able to*), about which you will find more information in the Language Reference Section.

| Vous pouvez | | *Can you?* | |
| Pourriez-vous | me rappeler? | *Could you* | *call me back?* |
| Il/Elle peut | | *Can he/she* | |

| Est-ce que je peux parler à M. Martin? | *Can I speak to M. Martin?* |

| Je peux rappeler? | *Can I call back?* |

# Language map

**Madame Prévost, s'il vous plaît.**

*La secrétaire de Madame Prévost à l'appareil.*

**Bonjour, madame. C'est Steve Hubert de la société Hubert Associates Ltd à Oxford. Je voudrais parler à Madame Prévost.**

*Madame Prévost est en réunion pour l'instant. Voulez-vous laisser un message?*

**Elle peut me rappeler cette après-midi?**

*Bien, monsieur. Pourriez-vous me répéter vos coordonnées?*

**Oui, c'est Steve Hubert de la société Hubert Associates Ltd.**

*Merci. Et quelle est votre numéro de téléphone?*

**19 44 865 250903**

*Madame Prévost est en réunion cette après-midi aussi. Est-ce que je peux vous être utile?*

**C'est au sujet de notre rendez-vous du 8 mars. Je voudrais changer la date.**

*Quelle date vous convient?*

**Le 9 mars, si possible, à quatorze heures du soir.**

*C'est entendu. Au revoir, monsieur.*

# Unit 3 *Arriving at reception*

**Checklist**   By the end of this Unit you should be able to:

- ❏  announce yourself at reception
- ❏  say you have an appointment
- ❏  say what time your appointment is for
- ❏  introduce your companion(s)
- ❏  accept/refuse refreshments politely
- ❏  greet your host(ess)
- ❏  answer a few standard questions about your health, your journey and so forth, with a few standard answers.

**Key words and phrases**
*for you to use*

## At reception

| | |
|---|---|
| J'ai/Nous avons rendez-vous avec Monsieur/Madame X | *I/We have an appointment with Mr/Mrs X* |
| J'ai rendez-vous à dix heures | *I have an appointment at 10 a.m.* |
| Voici ma carte | *Here is my card* |
| Un café? Volontiers! | *A coffee? Yes please!* |
| avec du sucre | *with sugar* |
| avec du lait | *with milk* |
| Je préfère le thé | *I prefer tea* |

## Meeting and greeting

| | |
|---|---|
| Comment allez-vous? | *How are you?* |
| Très bien, merci | *Very well, thank you* |
| Un peu fatigué(e) | *A little tired* |
| Le voyage? Pas trop mal/ Sans problèmes | *The journey? Not too bad/ No problems* |
| Je vous présente mon associé(e) | *Can I introduce you to my colleague?* |
| Enchanté(e)/Bonjour | *Pleased to meet you/Hello* |

## Excuses, excuses

| | |
|---|---|
| Je suis désolé(e)/Je m'excuse | *I'm sorry/I apologise* |
| la grêve! | *the strike!* |
| le retard! | *the delay!* |
| la circulation (intense)! | *the (heavy) traffic!* |

## Responding to apologies

| | |
|---|---|
| Ce n'est pas grave! | *It's not important!* |
| Ça ne fait rien! | *It doesn't matter!* |

**Key words and phrases**
*for you to recognize*

## At reception

| | |
|---|---|
| C'est à quel nom? | *Your name please?* |
| C'est de la part de qui? | |
| Comment? | *What did you say? (literally **how?**)* |
| Est-ce que je peux vous aider? | *Can I help you?* |
| A quelle heure avez-vous rendez-vous? | *At what time is your appointment?* |
| Voulez-vous vous asseoir? | *Would you like to have a seat?* |
| Pouvez-vous patienter quelques instants/encore un petit peu? | *Could you wait for a few minutes/a little longer?* |
| Je vais prévenir Monsieur X | *I'll let Mr X know you're here* |
| Je vais chercher Madame X | *I'll go and get Mrs X* |
| Monsieur X est encore en réunion | *Mr X is still in a meeting* |
| Il n'est pas encore rentré du déjeuner | *He isn't back from lunch yet* |
| Je peux vous offrir un café/thé? | *Can I offer you a coffee/tea?* |
| Vous prenez du sucre/du lait? | *Do you take sugar/milk?* |
| Vous préférez le thé peut-être? | *You prefer tea perhaps?* |

## Meeting and greeting

| | |
|---|---|
| Je m'excuse/Je suis désolé(e) de vous avoir fait attendre | *Sorry to have kept you waiting* |
| Je vous ai fait attendre? | *Have I kept you waiting?* |
| Vous avez fait bon voyage? | *Did you have a good journey?* |
| Vous avez trouvé nos bureaux sans difficulté? | *Did you find us (lit. **our offices**) without (too much) trouble?* |
| Si vous voulez me suivre, on va passer dans mon bureau | *If you would like to follow me, we'll go through to my office* |

## Excuses, excuses

| | |
|---|---|
| Une réunion/Un déjeuner interminable! | *An endless meeting/lunch!* |

**Pen and paper exercises**

1 Listen to the two receptionists talking about the visitors they expect, and complete the schedule. The visitors' names are listed below. Write the names in the appropriate spaces. Note that two visitors have an appointment at the same time.

Les visiteurs: Mme Grandet, Société Monnot
M. Foncet, EDF
M. Baudet, audit interne
Mme Saillard, agence de publicité

| lundi | 10 juin | |
|---|---|---|
| **Heure** | **Visiteur** | **Pour** |
| 10.30 | | *Mme Roche, service marketing* |
| | | *M Dupuis, service des achats* |
| 11.00 | | *M. Paget, service technique* |
| 11.30 | | *M Martin, comptabilité* |

2 Can you sort out this dialogue between June and the receptionist? June speaks first.

a) *June*: Les Wilcox et June Jones de Fenestral.

b) *June*: A onze heures, madame.

c) *Receptionist*: C'est de la part de qui, s'il vous plaît?

d) *June*: Voici ma carte.

e) *Receptionist*: Voulez-vous vous asseoir? Je vais prévenir M. Leroy.

f) *Receptionist*: Comment?

g) *June*: Bonjour, madame. Nous avons rendez-vous avec M. Leroy.

h) *Receptionist*: Merci. A quelle heure avez-vous rendez-vous?

**Language debrief**

## A share of the action (saying who is doing something)

English verbs generally have two present tense forms, whose use depends on who the doer is, e.g. *I speak*, but *she speaks*, *you work*, but *he works*.

It's rather like this in French, except that *almost every* doer (*I, you, he, she, it, we* or *they*) has his or her own form of the verb.

Sometimes the differences, which mostly involve changes in the way the word ends, are only in the spelling, and you just can't hear them when the words are spoken. In other cases the difference between the forms can be heard very clearly.

French verbs divide into several groups, each of which has typical forms. One of the biggest groups has a basic form (the form you find when you look in a dictionary) which ends in **-er**. Some verbs of this type which we have met so far are: **parler** (*to speak*), **confirmer** (*to confirm*), **regretter** (*to regret*).

Here are the different forms of these verbs for each person:

| *I* | je | parle | confirme | regrette |
| *he/she* | il/elle | parle | confirme | regrette |
| *they* | ils/elles | parlent | confirment | regrettent |

When spoken, the **-e** or **-ent** ending is silent, so all these forms sound the same.

| *we* | nous | parlons | confirmons | regrettons |
| *you* | vous | parlez | confirmez | regrettez |

In these cases the ending **-ons** or **-ez** is pronounced. Listen out for the correct pronunciation in examples on the tape.

The endings **-ons** and **-ez** are valid for other groups of verbs too, ones whose basic forms end in **-ir** or **-re**. However the forms for the other persons follow different patterns. We've given you an example of each in the Language Reference section.

## 'Having' and 'being'

Not a chapter from a philosophical treatise, but a note on two very common, but highly irregular verbs, **être** *(to be)* and **avoir** *(to have)*. Because they are so common you will no doubt learn them quickly, despite their irregularity.

Here are some of the contexts in which we have so far met these verbs. The complete list of forms is in the Language Reference Section.

**être**    Je **suis** Mark Dodsworth de la société LCI à Bath.

Je **suis** désolée, monsieur, mais M. Lebrun **est** en vacances.

Mme Tissot?  Elle **est** en réunion.

M. Wilcox et Mme Jones **sont** à la réception.

**avoir**    J'**ai** rendez-vous avec Mme Prévost.

Nous **avons** rendez-vous avec M. Leroy.

Elle **a** rendez-vous avec M. Dupuis.

## Handing something over

As you pass an object to someone, you say in French:

**Voici** ma carte             *Here's my card*
**Voici** notre brochure       *Here's our brochure*

## Pointing something out

Both **voici** and its partner **voilà** can be used to point out a person or object. The sales assistant in the department store says to Steve: **La voilà** (*There she is*), when she sees Mme Prévost approaching. When pointing out a man, she would have said: **Le voilà**.

Use **voici** to point out things close to you (*here is ......*) and **voilà** for things further away (*there is ......* ).

And no doubt you will hear **Voilà!** used as an exclamation denoting success: *I've done it!* Say it yourself when you've won a valuable contract!

## Being negative

Not an attitude we would wish to encourage, but sometimes it's necessary.

To say *not* use **ne ...... pas** or **n' ...... pas**, as in:

Ce **n'**est **pas** grave          *It's **not** serious*

Nous **n'**avons **pas** de lait     *We haven't any milk*

You'll find some more examples in the recording for Unit 4.

# Language map

*Monsieur, madame?*

**Bonjour, madame.
Nous avons rendez-vous
avec Monsieur Leroy.**

*C'est de la part de qui?*

**Monsieur Wilcox et Mme
Jones de la société
Fenestral.**

*A quelle heure avez-vous
rendez-vous?*

**Nous avons rendez-vous à
onze heures.**

*Voulez-vous vous asseoir?
Je vais prévenir Monsieur
Leroy.*

**Monsieur Leroy arrive
à la reception**

*Monsieur Wilcox,
comment allez-vous?*

**Très bien, merci.**

*Vous avez fait bon voyage?*

**Pas trop mal, merci. Je
vous présente mon
associée, Madame Jones.**

*Enchanté. Voulez-vous me
suivre? On va passer dans
mon bureau.*

*Je suis désolée, mais
Monsieur Leroy est encore
en réunion. Je peux vous
offrir un café?*

**Volontiers!**

*Vous le prenez comment?
Avec du sucre?*

**Oui, et avec du lait, aussi,
s'il vous plaît.**

*Monsieur Wilcox, je
m'excuse de vous avoir fait
attendre.*

**Ce n'est pas grave.**

# Unit 4   *Presenting your company and its products 1*

***Checklist***   By the end of this Unit you will have learnt:

❏ how to present yourself, your company and your products

❏ how to talk about dimensions

❏ how to talk about delivery terms and payment.

You will also learn a few basic strategies for meetings and to ask business–related questions in French as you go round the French company.

**Key words and phrases**
*for you to use*

## Introducing yourself and others

| | |
|---|---|
| Je suis/Je vous présente ...... le directeur/la directrice du service export | *I am/Let me introduce ...... the export manager* |

## Presenting the company

| | |
|---|---|
| Nous sommes une société de taille moyenne | *We are a medium-sized company* |
| Nous existons depuis cinquante ans | *We've been in business 50 years* |
| Nous fabriquons ...... | *We make ......* |
|    des fenêtres |    *windows* |
|    des pulls faits à la main |    *hand-made jumpers* |
|    x fenêtres/pulls par mois |    *x windows/jumpers a month* |
| Nous voulons exporter en France | *We want to export to France* |
| Nous nous spécialisons en/ dans ...... | *We specialize in ......* |
| Nous avons ...... | *We have ......* |
|    environ cent employés |    *about 100 employees* |
|    x pour cent du marché intérieur/hollandais |    *x % of the home market/ Dutch market* |
|    x unités de production |    *x production units* |
|    une grande gamme de produits |    *a large product range* |
| Nous avons l'intention de lancer un nouveau produit | *We intend to launch a new product* |
| Notre chiffre d'affaires est de 30 millions de francs | *Our turnover is 30 million francs* |

## Presenting the product

### Its quality

| | |
|---|---|
| C'est un produit ...... | *It's a ......* |
| de haute qualité | *high quality* |
| robuste | *strong* |
| moderne | *modern* |
| pratique | *practical product* |

### Its advantages

| | |
|---|---|
| Notre produit est facile ...... | *Our product is easy ......* |
| à installer | *to install* |
| à nettoyer | *to clean* |

### Its dimensions

| | |
|---|---|
| Notre produit fait 250 centimètres/millimètres ...... | *Our product is 250 cm./mm. ......* |
| de long | *long* |
| de large | *wide* |
| de haut | *tall* |
| de diamètre | *in diameter* |
| d'épaisseur | *thick* |

### What it's made of

| | |
|---|---|
| Notre produit est en ...... | *Our product is in/made of ......* |
| aluminium | *aluminium* |
| bois | *wood* |
| carton | *cardboard* |
| uPVC | *uPVC* |
| verre | *glass* |

## Price and delivery

| | |
|---|---|
| Nous fabriquons sur commande | *We make to order* |
| Voici une liste des prix | *Here is a price list* |
| Nous avons des prix intéressants | *We have attractive prices* |
| Il y a une remise de x pour cent | *There is a discount of x%* |

| | |
|---|---|
| Nos délais de livraison? | *How long do deliveries take?* |
| Un mois et demi/six semaines | *A month and a half/six weeks* |
| Nous préférons le crédit documentaire irrévocable | *We prefer (payment by) irrevocable letter of credit* |

## Tactical phrases for meetings

| | |
|---|---|
| C'est une question très intéressante! | *That's a very interesting question!* |
| Je vais me renseigner | *I'll find out* |
| Je vais vérifier au bureau | *I'll check with the office* |
| Nous avons vérifié | *We've checked* |
| Pardon! Un malentendu, sans doute | *Sorry! A misunderstanding, no doubt* |
| Si j'ai bien compris, vous voulez passer une commande | *If I've understood correctly, you want to place an order* |

## Asking business–related questions

| | |
|---|---|
| Vous achetez vos pièces dans la région? | *Do you buy your parts locally?* |
| Vous fabriquez vos propres pièces? | *Do you make your own parts?* |
| Vous avez vos propres camions? | *Do you have your own lorries?* |
| Vous travaillez avec de grandes entreprises? | *Do you work with big companies?* |
| Quels/Qui sont vos clients? | *Who are your clients?* |
| Combien de fournisseurs avez-vous? | *How many suppliers do you have?* |

## Useful expressions

| | |
|---|---|
| C'est vrai! | *It's true!/That's true!* |
| Ça va venir! | *That's coming!* |
| Ça dépend! | *It depends!* |
| Vous voyez? | *Do you see?* |

**Key words and phrases**
*for you to recognize*

## Understanding questions about your company

| | |
|---|---|
| Quel est votre chiffre d'affaires? | *What is your turnover?* |
| Quelle part du marché français avez-vous? | *What share of the French market do you have?* |
| Combien d'unités de fabrication avez-vous? | *How many production units do you have?* |
| Combien de fenêtres/ pulls fabriquez-vous par semaine/mois? | *How many windows/pullovers do you make per week/month?* |
| Avez-vous une grande gamme de produits? | *Do you have a big range of products?* |

## Understanding questions about your products

| | |
|---|---|
| Quelles sont les dimensions de votre produit? | *What are the dimensions of your product?* |
| Avez-vous beaucoup de modèles? tailles? | *Have you got lots of models? sizes?* |
| Vos produits sont en quelle matière? | *What are your products made of?* |
| Votre produit est conforme aux nouvelles normes européennes? | *Does your product conform to the new European standards?* |
| Est-ce que vous fournissez des pièces? | *Do you supply (spare) parts?* |

## Understanding questions about delivery terms and payment

| | |
|---|---|
| Vous avez beaucoup de produits en stock? | *Do you have lots of products in stock?* |
| Vous fabriquez sur commande? | *Do you manufacture to order?* |
| Vous avez une liste des prix? | *Do you have a price list?* |
| Vous faites des remises? | *Do you give discounts?* |
| Quels sont vos délais de livraison? | *How long do deliveries take?* |
| Quelles sont vos conditions de paiement? | *What are your terms of payment?* |
| Pouvez-vous nous faire un devis en francs français? | *Can you give us an estimate in French francs?* |

## Understanding your guide on the tour of the premises

| | |
|---|---|
| Ici vous avez la chaîne de production | *Here you have the production line* |
| A droite/A gauche nous avons la zone de stockage/d'emballage | *To the right/To the left we have the storage/ packing area* |
| Qu'est-ce que nous utilisons comme emballage?...... | *What do we use as packaging?......* |
| Je vais vous montrer ...... | *I'll show you ......* |

## Useful phrases to recognise

| | |
|---|---|
| Je m'en doutais! | *I thought as much!* |

**Pen and paper exercises**

1 Listen to June enumerating the benefits of Fenestral's windows and number the statements reprinted below in the order in which you hear them.

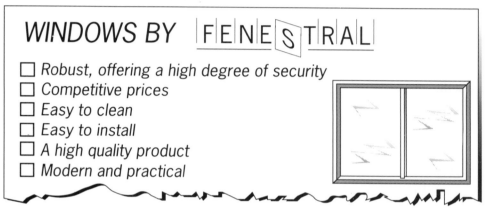

WINDOWS BY FENESTRAL

☐ Robust, offering a high degree of security
☐ Competitive prices
☐ Easy to clean
☐ Easy to install
☐ A high quality product
☐ Modern and practical

2 Listen to the conversations and fill in the dimensions.

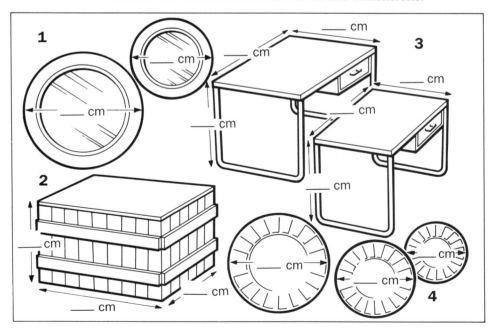

# Language map 1

## Presenting your company

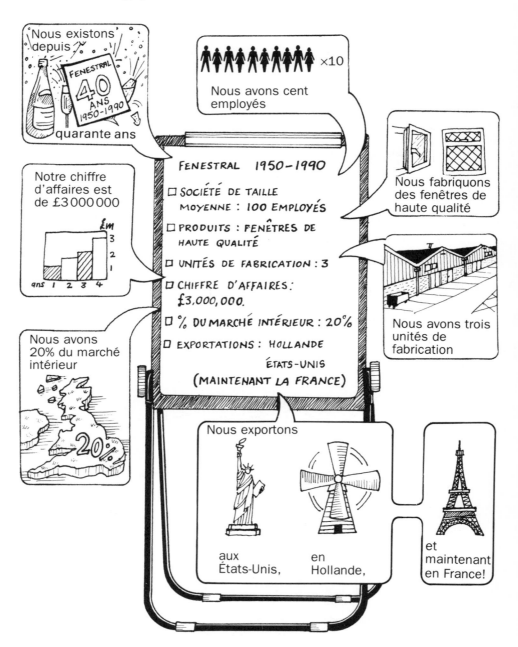

# Language map 2

## Presenting your product

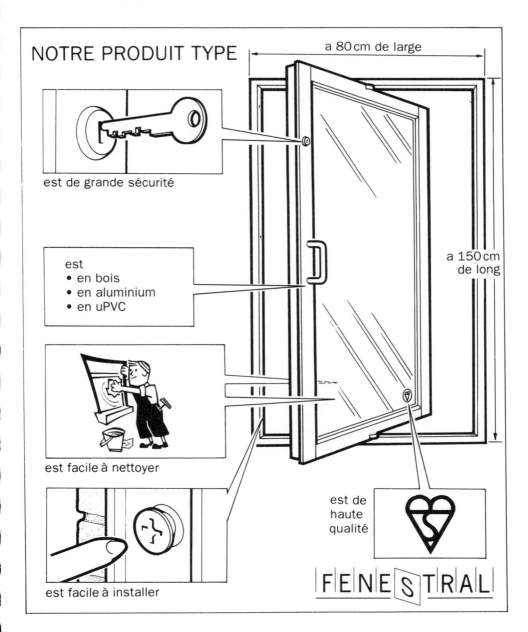

NOTRE PRODUIT TYPE

a 80 cm de large

a 150 cm de long

est de grande sécurité

est
• en bois
• en aluminium
• en uPVC

est facile à nettoyer

est facile à installer

est de haute qualité

FENESTRAL

# Language map 3

## Fixing the terms

**Language debrief**

## How long did you say?

Fenestral has been in existence for 40 years. June tells M. Leroy:

Nous existons **depuis** quarante ans.

Notice that in French we say *we exist* (**nous existons**) *for 40 years*, rather than *we have existed*. And if you want to say *since when* something has been happening, then **depuis** will do that job too:

Nous existons **depuis 1950** *We've been in existence **since 1950***

## Asking how many

| | |
|---|---|
| Combien de ...... ? | *How many ...... ?* |
| Combien de fenêtres fabriquez-vous par semaine? | *How many windows do you make each week?* |
| Combien d'employés avez-vous? | *How many workers do you have?* |

In both these cases the question is asked using the reversed word order - **fabriquez-vous, avez-vous**.

We can also ask such questions by using the normal word order. In this case the phrase with **combien de** is placed after the verb, e.g.

Vous fabriquez combien de fenêtres par semaine?

Vous avez combien d'employés?

Other questions involving question words can, of course, be asked in the same way, e.g.

Vous existez depuis quand? *Since when have you existed?*

49

## He, she, it and they

As you know, even inanimate objects like windows (**la fenêtre** : feminine) have a gender in French, so you will hear **il** and **elle** used when referring to objects as *it*.

| | |
|---|---|
| **Le bureau** est robuste | *The desk is strong* |
| **Il** est robuste | *It is strong* |
| **La fenêtre** est ronde | *The window is round* |
| **Elle** est ronde | *It is round* |

Unlike English, where we only have one plural form *(they)*, in French you have to distinguish between male and female in the plural too. Thus:

| | |
|---|---|
| **Les bureaux** sont robustes | **Ils** sont robustes |
| **Les fenêtres** sont rondes | **Elles** sont rondes |

## A word of many parts

In this Unit you have met the little word **en** in a variety of senses.

*in* or *to* **a country**:

| | |
|---|---|
| Nous vendons bien **en** Hollande | *We're selling well **in** Holland* |
| Nous voulons exporter **en** France | *We want to export **to** France* |

But note: **aux** Etats-Unis

**made of a particular material**:

| | |
|---|---|
| des fenêtres **en** uPVC / **en** bois | *windows **made of** uPVC / wood* |

**And in answer to the question**:

| | |
|---|---|
| Combien d'employés avez-vous? | *How many employees do you have?* |

**you might reply**:

| | |
|---|---|
| Nous **en** avons mille | *We have a thousand (**of them**)* |

Listen to the tape for more examples of these different meanings of **en**.

## Talking about dimensions

There is a standard pattern you can use to express the dimensions of an object, as follows:

| Il/elle fait ...... cm ...... | *It's ...... cm ......* |
|---|---|
| de long | *long* |
| de large | *wide* |
| de haut | *high/tall* |
| de diamètre | *in diameter* |
| d'épaisseur | *thick* |

## Describing people and objects

When in English we use a word to describe a person or an object (in grammatical terms, an adjective), we place it before that person or thing, e.g. a *robust* model, a *typical* window. In French you can do this with a few common words, but in most cases you must place the adjective after the word it describes, e.g.

| une fenêtre **type** | *a **typical** window* |
| un modèle **robuste** | *a **robust** model* |

Some of the adjectives that go before the noun are:

| une **grande/petite** fenêtre | *a **large/small** window* |
| un **bon/nouveau/vieux** modèle | *a **good/new/old** model* |

51

# Unit 5 *Presenting your company and its products 2*

**Checklist**

In this Unit you will learn more about:

❑ presenting yourself, your company and your product.

You will also learn:

❑ how to ask and answer questions about the market

❑ how to talk in percentages.

## Section 1  **Key words and phrases**
*for you to use*

### Introducing yourself

Je suis la directrice/le directeur
d'une petite entreprise
familiale

*I am the director
of a small family business*

### Talking about your workforce

Nous employons des équipes
de travailleurs (à domicile)
spécialisés

*We employ teams of
specialized (home-based)
workers*

### Talking about your products

La qualité de nos produits
est garantie

*The quality of our products
is guaranteed*

### Talking about your company's performance

Nos ventes cette année
ont augmenté de cinquante
pour cent

*Our sales this year
have increased by 50%*

par rapport à l'année dernière

*compared to last year*

Nous vendons très bien
aux Etats-Unis/au Japon/
en Allemagne

*We are selling very well
in the States/in Japan/
in Germany*

### Talking about your customers

Les Français, comme les
Américains, apprécient la
qualité

*The French, like the Americans
appreciate quality*

## Researching the market for your product

| | |
|---|---|
| Vous vendez combien de pulls écossais ...... | *How many Scottish pullovers do you sell ......* |
|    par semaine? | *per week?* |
|    par mois? | *per month?* |
|    par an? | *per year?* |
| Quel est votre client type? | *Who is your typical client?* |
| Quelles tailles se vendent bien? | *Which sizes sell well?* |
| Est-ce que nos modèles sont bien adaptés au marché français? | *Are our models well suited to the French market?* |

## Talking about delivery terms and payment

| | |
|---|---|
| Nous livrons par colis postal recommandé | *We deliver by registered post* |
| Vous payez contre facture | *You pay against invoice* |

## Au revoir! (taking your leave)

| | |
|---|---|
| Voici ma carte/notre brochure/des échantillons | *Here is my card/our brochure/some samples* |
| Je vous remercie de votre accueil/visite | *Thank you for your welcome/visit* |
| C'est moi qui vous remercie de votre visite/accueil | *It's I who should thank you for your visit/welcome* |

## Useful expressions

| | |
|---|---|
| C'est exact/C'est cela! | *That's right!* |
| Pourquoi pas? | *Why not?* |
| Normalement | *Usually* |
| C'est noté | *That's noted* |

**Key words and phrases**
*for you to recognize*

## Understanding the hype

| | |
|---|---|
| Nous avons beaucoup de succès avec nos produits dans tous les pays européens | *We are doing very well with our products in all the European countries* |
| Nous sommes maintenant une compagnie de dimension internationale avec siège social à Bruxelles | *We are now a company operating on an international scale with headquarters at Brussels* |
| Notre chiffre d'affaires l'année dernière a dépassé un milliard de francs | *Our turnover last year exceeded one thousand million francs* |
| Nous avons *x* filiales à l'étranger | *We have x branches abroad* |
| Notre croissance a été très rapide | *Our growth has been very rapid* |
| Nous n'avons pas beaucoup de concurrence | *We haven't got much competition* |

## Understanding what the buyer says

**About the market**

| | |
|---|---|
| En hiver nous vendons mieux qu'en été | *In winter we sell better than in summer* |
| Notre client type? | *Our typical client?* |
| C'est une mère de famille qui offre un pull à sa fille | *It's a mother buying her daughter a pullover* |
| Les tailles qui se vendent bien? ...... Le trente-huit et le quarante | *The sizes which sell well? ...... 38 and 40* |

### About your products

| | |
|---|---|
| J'aime beaucoup vos produits | *I like your products very much* |
| Ils sont très intéressants et originaux ...... (mais) les couleurs ne sont pas assez vives | *They're very interesting and original ...... (but) the colours are not bright enough* |

## Queries and requests from the buyer

| | |
|---|---|
| Vous pouvez me laisser quelques échantillons? | *Can you leave me some samples?* |
| Quel est le prix des pièces (détachées)? | *What is the price of (spare) parts?* |
| Vous avez toutes les pièces en stock? | *Do you have all the parts in stock?* |
| Vous confirmez le devis par lettre? | *Will you confirm the quote by letter?* |

1  Listen to the interviews and complete the company profiles.

○  <u>*HÉLÈNE HERNAUD*</u> – *PRODUITS DE BEAUTÉ*

<u>*FOUNDED:*</u> . . . . . *YEARS AGO*
<u>*HEAD OFFICE:*</u>
<u>*MANUFACTURING PLANTS IN:*</u>

○  <u>*TOTAL N⁰ OF EMPLOYEES*</u>:
<u>*IN FRANCE :*</u>
<u>*TURNOVER LAST YEAR:*</u>
<u>*CURRENT MARKET:*</u>

○  <u>*FUTURE PLANS :*</u>

<u>*AGENCE DE PUBLICITÉ MARTIN*</u>

<u>*FOUNDED:*</u> . . . . . *YEARS AGO*
<u>*BRANCHES IN:*</u>

<u>*N⁰ OF EMPLOYEES IN FRANCE:*</u>
<u>*ABROAD:*</u>

○  <u>*TURNOVER LAST YEAR:*</u>

2  Listen to the interview and fill in the percentage represented by each segment.

**Proportion of turnover in various markets**

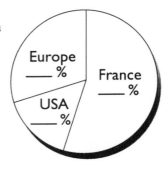

Europe ___ %

France ___ %

USA ___ %

The shaded areas represent the rate of increase in each market.
Insert the figures.

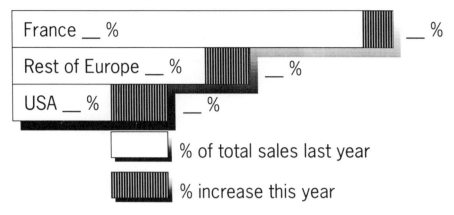

France __ %     __ %

Rest of Europe __ %     __ %

USA __ %     __ %

[ ] % of total sales last year

% increase this year

**3** Listen to the conversation and complete the notes.

| | AX45 | AX32 |
|---|---|---|
| In stock? | | |
| Delivery dates? | | |
| Price? | | |
| Do they give discounts? | | |
| %? | | |
| method of payment? | | |

# Language map 1

## *New markets*

Nous avons une grande gamme de produits . . .

Nos ventes cette année ont augmenté de cent pour cent . . .

Nous vendons très bien en Angleterre en, Italie et en Allemagne . . .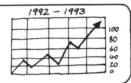

Maintenant nous voulons exporter au Japon.

# Language map 2

## Researching the market

Vous vendez
combien
de pulls par mois?

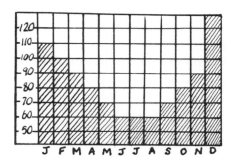

Ça dépend. 50 ou
60 environ.
En hiver nous
vendons
mieux qu'en été.

Qui est votre
client type?

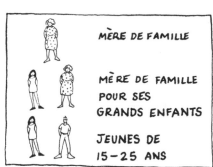

MÈRE DE FAMILLE

MÈRE DE FAMILLE
POUR SES
GRANDS ENFANTS

JEUNES DE
15 – 25 ANS

C'est une mère de
famille qui offre un
pull à sa fille . . .

Quelles tailles se
vendent bien?

| cm | | |
|----|----|----|
| 36 | | |
| 38 | ✓ | |
| 40 | ✓ | |
| 42 | | |
| 44 | | |
| 46 | | |

Le trente-huit et
le quarante, surtout.

Est-ce que ces
modèles sont bien
adaptés au marché
français?

| COULEUR | PRIX | STYLE | |
|---------|------|-------|------|
| | ✓ | ✓ | BIEN |
| | | | ASSEZ |
| ✓ | | | MAL |

Oui, mais les
couleurs ne sont
pas assez vives.

**Language debrief**

## Goods that sell themselves

If only they did! Unfortunately it happens only in a grammatical sense. Mme Hernaud said:

Nos produits **se** vendent
bien en France

*Our products sell **themselves**
well in France.*

However, if you talk about a person or a company selling goods, the the word **se** disappears, e.g.

Nous vendons nos
produits en France.

*We sell our goods
in France.*

## Talking percentages

To express a percentage in French is very straightforward:

cinq pour cent:  5%          vingt pour cent:  20%

Our various speakers talk about percentages in several contexts. Firstly in saying what percentage of a particular market they have:

Nous avons 20% du
marché intérieur

*We have 20% of the
home market*

Secondly, in saying what percentage of production is sold where:

Nous vendons 53% de
notre production dans le
marché intérieur

*We sell 53% of our
production in the
home market*

In talking about percentage increases of sales:

Nos ventes ont augmenté
de 30% par rapport à
l'année dernière

*Our sales have increased
30% in comparison with
last year*

And finally in reference to discounts:

Il y a une remise de 5%

*There's a discount of 5%*

## Making comparisons

Steve refers to the discounts available on an order for more than 10 sweaters - une commande **de plus de** dix pulls.

| **plus de** | *more than* |
|---|---|
| **moins de** | *less than* |

These are the phrases to use when you are comparing numbers or amounts of money.

In other comparisons use **plus que, moins que, mieux que,** etc, e.g.

| Nous vendons plus que la concurrence | *We sell more than our competitors* |
|---|---|
| En hiver nous vendons mieux qu'en été | *In winter we sell better than in summer* |

## Asking how

| Comment ...... ? | *How ...... ?* |
|---|---|

This is another question word that is frequently placed after the verb, rather than at the beginning of the questions, e.g.

| Vous livrez comment? | *How do you deliver?* |
|---|---|
| On paie comment? | *How does one pay?* |

## Asking about price

There are two ways of asking how much something costs. Either ask:

| Quel est le prix de ...... ? | *What is the price of ...... ?* |
|---|---|

Or:

| Ça coûte combien? | *What does this cost?* |
|---|---|

# Unit 6 *Eating out with business contacts*

**Checklist**    In this Unit you will learn to:

❏   order food and drink in a restaurant

❏   ask what things are, what is recommended
     and what is available

❏   say what you like and dislike.

You will also learn some small talk for the
dinner table.

**Key words and phrases**
*for you to use*

## Asking for help or information

| | |
|---|---|
| Le Ricard? Qu'est-ce que c'est? | *Ricard? What's that?* |
| Qu'est-ce que vous avez comme fromage/vin/dessert? | *What do you have in the way of cheese/wine/dessert?* |
| Vous avez des vins de la région? | *Do you have any local wines?* |
| Qu'est-ce que vous me conseillez? | *What do you recommend?* |

## Ordering and paying

| | |
|---|---|
| Je prends un pâté canard | *I'll have a duck pâté* |
| Je voudrais un steak à point | *I'll have a medium steak* |
| L'addition, je vous prie | *The bill, please* |
| C'est combien? | *How much is that?* |

## Accepting/refusing

| | |
|---|---|
| Volontiers! | *Yes, please!* |
| Je veux bien! | *I wouldn't mind!* |
| Je veux bien goûter les fruits de mer | *I wouldn't mind trying the seafood* |
| Je ne dis pas non! | *I won't say no!* |
| C'est très gentil de votre part! | *It's very kind of you!* |
| Merci! J'ai assez mangé! | *No thanks! I've eaten enough!* |
| Pas pour moi! | *Not for me!* |

## Expressing likes and dislikes

| | |
|---|---|
| J'aime (beaucoup) la cuisine française | *I like French cooking (very much)* |
| Je n'aime pas les fruits de mer | *I don't like seafood* |
| Je préfère l'eau minérale gazeuse | *I prefer fizzy mineral water* |
| J'adore les frites/la pâtisserie | *I love chips/patisserie* |

## Business talk

| | |
|---|---|
| Demain? Je vais à New York | *Tomorrow? I'm going to New York* |
| J'ai rendez-vous avec ...... | *I have an appointment with ......* |
| Je rentre en Angleterre | *I'm going back to England* |

## Small talk

### Talking about yourself

| | |
|---|---|
| Je suis marié(e) | *I'm married* |
| Je ne suis pas marié(e) | *I'm not married* |
| J'ai deux enfants | *I have two children* |
| Je n'ai pas d'enfants | *I have no children* |
| Je suis de Sheffield/Glasgow | *I'm from Sheffield/Glasgow* |
| J'habite Londres/Manchester | *I live in London/Manchester* |
| Je fume/Je ne fume pas | *I smoke/I do not smoke* |
| Je travaille pour ...... depuis x ans | *I've been working for ...... for x years* |
| Je voyage beaucoup | *I travel a lot* |

### Talking about the weather

| | |
|---|---|
| Il fait beau/chaud/froid | *It's fine/hot/cold* |
| Il pleut/Il neige | *It's raining/It's snowing* |

## Section 2 **Key words and phrases**
*for you to recognize*

### Table talk

| | | |
|---|---|---|
| **The invitation** | Voulez-vous dîner avec nous? | *Would you like to have dinner with us?* |
| | Je passerai vous prendre toute à l'heure/ à huit heures | *I'll come and pick you up in a little while/ at 8 o'clock* |
| **Before the meal** | Vous voulez boire quelque chose? | *Would you like something to drink?* |
| | Vous prenez un apéritif? | *Will you have an aperitif?* |
| | Je vous le mets sur la note? | *Shall I put in on the bill?* |
| | Cette table vous convient? | *Does this table suit you?* |
| | Vous désirez le menu ou la carte? | *Would you like the (fixed) menu or the à la carte menu?* |
| **Discussing the menu** | Voulez-vous goûter une spécialité de la maison? | *Would you like to taste a speciality of the house?* |
| | Aimez-vous le pâté? | *Do you like pâté?* |
| | Je vous conseille le poisson | *I recommend the fish* |
| | Je vous propose la viande | *I suggest you try the meat* |
| | C'est un plat/vin typique de la région | *It's a typical dish/wine of the region* |
| **Ordering the meal** | Vous avez choisi? | *Have you chosen?* |
| | Pour commencer? Comme entrée? | *To start with? As a starter?* |
| | Comme plat principal/ dessert? | *As a main course/dessert?* |
| | Vous préférez le steak à point ou saignant? | *Do you prefer the steak medium or rare?* |
| | Bon appétit! | *Have a good meal!* |

## Business talk

| | |
|---|---|
| Ça marche, les affaires? | *Is business going well?* |
| Vous travaillez pour Fenestral depuis longtemps? | *Have you been working for Fenestral for long?* |
| Vous êtes content(e) de votre visite chez nous? | *Are you pleased with your visit to us?* |
| Vous rentrez en Angleterre demain, n'est-ce pas? | *You're going back to England tomorrow, aren't you?* |

## Small talk

### General

| | |
|---|---|
| Vous connaissez la France?/ la Bretagne? | *Do you know France?/Brittany?* |
| C'est votre première visite à Nantes? | *Is it your first visit to Nantes?* |
| Vous êtes d'où? | *Where are you from?* |
| Vous habitez où? | *Where do you live?* |
| Ça vous dérange si je fume? | *Do you mind if I smoke?* |
| C'est vrai qu'il pleut tout le temps en Angleterre? | *Is it true that it rains all the time in England?* |
| C'est vrai que les Anglais mangent le fromage après le dessert? | *Is it true that the English eat cheese after the dessert?* |

### Personal

| | |
|---|---|
| Si je peux me permettre ...... | *If I may be so bold ......* |
| vous êtes marié(e)? | *are you married?* |
| vous avez des enfants? | *have you got children?* |
| c'est quoi, votre prénom? | *what is your first name?* |

**Pen and paper exercises**

1   Listen to the conversation in the restaurant and tick those items
    on the menu which you hear mentioned.

## Entrées et Salades

**Assiette de Coquillages et Crustaces**
Plate of mixed shellfish

**Plateau de Fruits de Mer**
Seafood platter

**Saumon Fumé**
Smoked salmon

**Terrine de Foie Gras de Canard**
Duck liver pâté

**Salade d'Artichaut Breton**
Salad of Breton artichokes

**Salade Mer et Jardin**
Seafood and vegetable salad

## Les Poissons

**Merlu à la sauce normande**
Hake in Normandy sauce

**Colin au beurre blanc**
Hake with butter sauce

**Colin au bleu**
Poached trout

2   Listen to the conversations between Mlle Prunier and Les, and between June and M. Leroy, and then answer the questions.

1   How old are Les's children?

2   What is his wife's job? Does she work for Fenestral?

3   How long has Les been working for Fenestral?

4   Where does June live?

5   Does she have any children?

## Viandes et Volailles

**Côte de Boeuf à l'Os**
Rib of beef on the bone

**Châteaubriand Sauce Béarnaise**
Châteaubriand with Bearnaise sauce

**Volaille fermière de Challons**
Chicken with vegetables in a cream sauce

## Les Fromages

**Plateau de fromages**
Cheese board

## Les desserts

**Glaces: parfums au choix**
Ice-cream: various flavours

**Tartelettes maison**
Home made fruit tartlets

**Corbeille de fruits de saison**
Selection of fresh fruit

**Language debrief**

## Asking what something is

Menus in other countries are full of unfamiliar things, so if you are going to sample fully the local cuisine, it's important to be able to ask what something is. The question you need in French is:

**Qu'est-ce que c'est?**

It may look complicated, but you just need to learn it as a set phrase. For the correct pronunciation listen to the early part of the Unit where Les is asking about **le pâté de canard**.

## Asking what is available

Qu'est-ce que vous avez comme | vin?
| voiture?

Literally: *What do you have in the way of* | *wine?*
| *car?*

or: *What sort of* | *wine* | *do you have?*
| *a car* |

This is a useful expression if you want to find out what is available within a particular category.
If you want to be more specific you can say:

| Quels vins avez-vous? | *What wines do you have?* |
| Quelle voiture avez-vous? | *What car do you have?* |

## Isn't that right?

You may remember M. Prévost says:

Ma femme est de Quimper, n'est-ce pas, chérie?

*My wife is from Quimper, isn't that right, darling?*

**N'est-ce pas** is a very useful phrase meaning *isn't that right?* It serves the same purpose as all those little questions like ...... *isn't it?*, ...... *don't you?*, ...... *shouldn't we?*, and so on, which we tag onto statements in English.

So if you were visibly enjoying your **fruits de mer** or **pâté de canard**, your French host might say:

Vous aimez la cuisine française, n'est-ce pas?
*You like French cooking, don't you?*

# Language map

**L'invitation**

*Voulez-vous dîner avec nous?*

**C'est très gentil de votre part!**

**Au restaurant**

*Vous prenez un apéritif?*

**Volontiers!**

*Voulez-vous goûter une spécialité de la maison?*

**Je veux bien. Qu'est-ce que vous me conseillez?**

*Aimez-vous le pâté? Le pâté maison est très bon.*

**Oui. J'adore le pâté.**

*Et après, je vous propose le colin.*

**Le colin, qu'est-ce que c'est?**

*C'est un poisson typique de la région.*

**Je suis désolé(e). Je n'aime pas le poisson.**

*Un steak alors? Vous préférez le steak à point ou saignant?*

**A point. Non, bien cuit, s'il vous plaît.**

**Plus tard au restaurant**

*Ça marche, les affaires?*

**Oui, oui, ça marche.**

*Vous travaillez pour Fenestral depuis longtemps?*

**Depuis trois ans.**

*Vous êtes content de votre visite chez nous?*

**Très content.
A notre collaboration!**

*Si je peux me permettre, vous êtes marié?*

**Oui, je suis marié.**

*Vous avez des enfants?*

**Oui, j'ai deux enfants.**

*Vous êtes d'où?*

**Je suis de Birmingham.**

*Il fait beau à Birmingham?*

**Non, il pleut beaucoup!**

*Un petit digestif?*

**Je ne dis pas non. Qu'est-ce que vous avez comme digestif?**

*Un cognac, un calvados.*

**Un cognac, alors.**

*Et une cigare?*

**Merci! Je ne fume pas.**

# Doing business in France

French business style tends to be quite formal, although this is changing somewhat amongst younger executives.

## Dos and Don'ts

**Do shake hands** when meeting someone and again when taking leave. This is a ritual that is repeated at every meeting, even amongst business colleagues who see each other every day. If there are a number of people present, go round everyone or risk being considered rude.

**Do praise French 'cuisine'** and be prepared to talk in some detail about food and wine. The French enjoy good conversation over a meal, about politics and culture as well as food and wine! The quick (sometimes alcohol-free) lunch in the canteen, or even a sandwich, is becoming more common in Paris but in the rest of France (or 'la province') lunch is still a full meal, consumed in a leisurely fashion, at home or in a restaurant.

**Do use the French you have learned** on this course but, until you have become really fluent, take along an interpreter or someone who knows French really well, if at all possible.

**Don't use first names.** Address your business acquaintance as Monsieur X or Madame X. Even people who have worked together for years use this formal form of address in France. People you don't know are simply 'monsieur' or 'madame'; to use no form of address sounds rude.

**Don't arrive exactly on time** if invited to someone's house for an evening meal. It's polite to be 15-20 minutes late. Don't take wine either; the French like to choose a wine to complement the food. Take flowers for your hostess instead, but not chrysanthemums (they're for funerals!). On the whole, though, the French tend to entertain in restaurants rather than at home.

**Don't try to do business in August.** Business goes very quiet from mid-July to September in France as people take 4-5 weeks annual leave, usually in one block, during this period.

**Don't wear your zany tie or city shorts!** The French tend to dress smartly but conservatively.

# What next?

Here are some further suggestions for improving your French and your knowledge of France.

**Enrol for some language training** to supplement your private study. Even a small number of hours of tuition will boost your confidence and allow you to clarify any points that may have been troubling you. Your local college or polytechnic may run courses for business people or offer tutor support, on a one-to-one basis, for students using open-learning packs like **French *Just for Business***. There are also many private organizations offering language training. The Association of Language Export Centres (Tel: 081-224 3748) is a useful source of information on good quality courses.

**Listen to the French radio** (for example, *France Inter* which has news flashes every half hour) and watch French films. If you have satellite TV, the possibilities are endless!

**Buy a French newspaper** such as *Le Figaro,* or a magazine such as *Paris-Match* or *L'Express* once a week. Even if you only understand the headlines or the gist of the articles you will acquire some useful French vocabulary.

**Improve your background knowledge** of France by working your way through a software package on doing business with the French called "Getting down to Business with France" (obtained from the Insurance Industrial Training Council, 90 Kippington Rd, Sevenoaks, Kent TN13 2LL. Tel: 0732-45080) or by reading the *Country Profile* on France published by the DTI. (Exports to Europe Branch, Department of Trade and Industry, 1 Victoria Street, London SW1H OET).

*Bonne chance!*

# Answers to exercises

## Unit 1

**1** 1. b   2. c   3. d   4. a

**2** 1. Dieudonné, Rochechouart   2. Benoit, Preignac

**3** 1. True   2. True   3. False   4. False

**4** The only time when you are both available is this afternoon, i.e. Monday afternoon.

## Unit 2

**1** 1. Correct   2. 45 14 48 23   3. Correct   4. 44 09 92 26

**3** Message 1: C (ii)   Message 2: A (iii)   Message 3: B (iv)

**4** 1. The message is from M. Logeay of Carrière; he wants to talk to Mrs Phillips about next week's meeting.
2. Mrs Cartwright's meeting tomorrow with M. Amieux, the head of the Export Department has been cancelled.
3. M. Leroy is arriving tomorrow, Tuesday, at 1.20 pm on flight BA254.

**5** You heard the recorded messages in the order 3, 4, 2, 1.

## Unit 3

**1** 10.30   Mme Saillard to see Mme Roche
and   Mme Grandet to see M. Dupuis
11.00   M. Foncet to see M. Paget
11.30   M. Baudet to see M. Martin

**2** The correct order is:  g, c, a, f, d, h, b, e

## Unit 4

**1** The order of the statements is:
A high quality product
Robust, offering a high degree of security
Modern and practical
Easy to install
Easy to clean

2  The dimensions are:
1.  Small window: 80 cm diameter;  large: 110 cm diameter.
2.  Crate: 90 cm long, 70cm wide, 50 cm high.
3.  Large desk:145 cm long, 75 cm wide, 72 cm high
    Small desk:130 cm long, 65 cm wide, 72 cm high.
4.  Large plate: 28 cm diameter;  medium:  23 cm;
    small: 18 cm.

## Unit 5

1  **Hélène Hernaud**
Founded 12 years ago; Head office in Marseilles; manufacturing
plants in France (2), Greece and Portugal;  680 employees in
total, 450 of them in France;  turnover last year was over 560
million francs; current markets Europe and USA; future plans:
to export to Japan.

**Agence de publicité Martin**
Founded 7 years ago; branches in Munich, Milan and London;
75 employees in France, 45 in other European countries;
turnover last year: 130 million francs.

2  Proportion of turnover in various markets: home market 53%;
rest of Europe 29%;  USA 18%.

Percentage increase in sales:  in France 5%;  in rest of Europe
16%;  in USA 30%.

3

|  | *AX 45* | *AX 32* |
|---|---|---|
| In stock? | Yes | Made to order |
| Delivery? | 15 days | $1 \frac{1}{2}$ months |
| Price? | 160 francs | 230 francs |

*Discounts*:  2% on orders of more than 200 000 francs; 5% on
orders of more than 500 000 francs.
*Payment*:  irrevocable documentary letter of credit.

## Unit 6

1  The items mentioned are:
le plateau de fruits de mer; la salade d'artichaut breton;
la terrine de foie gras de canard; le colin au beurre blanc;
le châteaubriand.

2  1. His son is 9 and his daughter 7.
2. His wife is a secretary.  She doesn't work for Fenestral.
3. 3 years.
4. In a small village near High Wycombe.
5. Yes, a little girl.

# Language reference

## Accents

In written French you will sometimes find one of three *accents* above the vowels, i.e. the letters **a, e, i, o** and **u**. They are described as *acute* ('), *grave* (`), and *circumflex* (^).

In the case of **é** and **è** they indicate a particular way of pronouncing the vowel: **é** is pronounced rather like a short, tight 'ay' in a word like 'say', as in **société**; **è** sounds like the 'e' of 'red', as in **après-midi.**

Sometimes an accent helps to distinguish between two words which would otherwise have the same spelling, e.g. **ou** (or) and **où** (where), or **a** (has) and **à** (to, at).

You'll also meet words that include **â, ê, î, ô** and **û**. These accents do not normally affect pronunciation.

## Pronunciation guide

As you become more familiar with the relationship between the spelling of a French word and its sound you will realize that many letters in the written word are redundant when it is spoken; as, for instance, the **w** is in the English word 'write'. This may seem confusing at first, but the ways in which this happens are very regular and you will soon recognize and learn them.

In this section we want to give you some tips for relating spelling to pronunciation, as we assume that you will want to use a dictionary to find words you need which do not occur in this course. These do not aim to be exhaustive, but to help you avoid the worst errors. For the precise pronunciation of individual sounds, listen carefully to the tape and imitate it as closely as possible.

1   The letter **-e** at the end of a word is not pronounced, e.g. **commence, achète.**

2   The group **-ent** at the end of a verb is not pronounced, e.g. **ils commencent, elles achètent.**

3   Single consonants or groups of consonants at the end of a word are silent, e.g. the **-t** in **il veut**, the group **-ds** in **je comprends.**

4   If an **-e** is added to a word ending in a silent consonant, e.g. to make it feminine (see note on adjectives), the consonant is then pronounced. For example, in the word **grand** the **-d** is silent, but in **grande** it is heard. (See also note on *liaison* below.)

5   If **n** or **m** follows a vowel it has a nasal sound, as in **en, nom, avons, dans, un**. But in words like **une** or **madame**, the final **-e** causes the **n** or **m** to be pronounced like the English equivalent.

6   In the **-ille** group of words, the double *l*s sound like the English *y*, e.g. **fille, travaille**. Two exceptions to this are **ville** (town) and **mille** (a thousand) where they are sounded as *l*s.

7   The letters **-é, -ée, -et, -er, -ez** at the end of a word are all pronounced like **-é** (see note on *Accents* above).

8   The letter **c** is pronounced like English *s* if it is followed by **e** or **i** or is written **ç**. Otherwise it is pronounced like English *k*.

## Liaison

No doubt sometimes when you hear French a whole sentence can sound like one enormously long word: it's difficult to tell where the boundaries between individual words are!

One reason for this is the fact that a letter at the end of a word which is normally silent **is** pronounced if the following word begins with a vowel.

So, for example, the **s** of **des** is not usually heard, as in **le service des ventes**, but it is pronounced in **le service des achats**, because of the **a** which follows it. Listen to these phrases on the tape. They occur early in Unit 1.

Similarly, the **d** of **quand** is normally silent. But you *do* hear it, pronounced in fact like a **t**, in the question: **Quand est-ce que je peux le rappeler?**

## Numbers (les nombres)

| | | | | | |
|---|---|---|---|---|---|
| 1 | un, une | 11 | onze | 21 | vingt et un |
| 2 | deux | 12 | douze | 22 | vingt-deux |
| 3 | trois | 13 | treize | 23 | vingt-trois |
| 4 | quatre | 14 | quatorze | 24 | vingt-quatre |
| 5 | cinq | 15 | quinze | 25 | vingt-cinq |
| 6 | six | 16 | seize | 26 | vingt-six |
| 7 | sept | 17 | dix-sept | 27 | vingt-sept |
| 8 | huit | 18 | dix-huit | 28 | vingt-huit |
| 9 | neuf | 19 | dix-neuf | 29 | vingt-neuf |
| 10 | dix | 20 | vingt | | |

| 30 | trente |
|---|---|
| 40 | quarante |
| 50 | cinquante |
| 60 | soixante |

For intermediate numbers, follow the pattern for 21-29

| | | | |
|---|---|---|---|
| 70 | soixante-dix | 80 | quatre-vingts |
| 71 | soixante et onze | 81 | quatre-vingt-un |
| 72 | soixante-douze | 82 | quatre-vingt-deux, etc. |
| 73 | soixante-treize | | |
| 74 | soixante-quatorze | 90 | quatre-vingt-dix |
| 75 | soixante-quinze | 91 | quatre-vingt-onze |
| 76 | soixante-seize | 92 | quatre-vingt-douze, etc. |
| 77 | soixante-dix-sept | | |
| 78 | soixante-dix-huit | | |
| 79 | soixante-dix-neuf | | |

| | | | |
|---|---|---|---|
| 100 | cent | 1000 | mille |
| 101 | cent un | 500 000 | cinq cent mille |
| 125 | cent vingt-cinq | 1 000 000 | un million |

20 350 000    vingt millions trois cent cinquante mille

## Time (l'heure)

| | |
|---|---|
| Quelle heure est-il? | *What time is it?* |
| neuf heures cinq | 9.05 |
| huit heures et quart<br>(*or* huit heures quinze) | 8.15 |
| onze heures et demie<br>(*or* onze heures trente ) | 11.30 |
| sept heures moins vingt<br>(*or* six heures quarante) | 6.40 |
| dix heures moins le quart<br>(*or* neuf heures quarante-cinq) | 9.45 |
| trois heures vingt de l'après-midi<br>(*or* quinze heures vingt) | 15.20 |
| Le rendez-vous est<br>à quelle heure? | *At what time is the appointment?* |
| Il est à dix heures trente | *It's at 10.30* |

## Days of the week (les jours de la semaine)

| | | | |
|---|---|---|---|
| lundi | *Monday* | vendredi | *Friday* |
| mardi | *Tuesday* | samedi | *Saturday* |
| mercredi | *Wednesday* | dimanche | *Sunday* |
| jeudi | *Thursday* | | |

## Months (les mois)

| | | | |
|---|---|---|---|
| janvier | *January* | juillet | *July* |
| février | *February* | août | *August* |
| mars | *March* | septembre | *September* |
| avril | *April* | octobre | *October* |
| mai | *May* | novembre | *November* |
| juin | *June* | décembre | *December* |

## The date (la date)

| | |
|---|---|
| Quelle est la date? | *What is the date?* |
| C'est ...... | *It's ......* |
|    le premier mars | *1st March* |
|    le neuf juin | *9th June* |
|    le vingt et un août | *21st August* |

The ordinal number is used only for the first of the month. For all other dates use the cardinal number.

| | |
|---|---|
| Quand avez-vous rendez-vous avec Fenestral? | *When do you have an appointment with Fenestral?* |
| J'ai rendez-vous le dix-huit octobre. | *I have an appointment on 18th October.* |

Note that in the above sentence the word *on* is not rendered in French.

## Telephone numbers (les numéros de téléphone)

French telephone numbers always have eight digits, of which the first two are the area code.

If you are dialling France from England, preface the 8-digit number with 010 33.

If you are dialling a French number within France:

1 Within the same dialling code area simply dial the 8-digit number.

2 To dial Paris from another area, preface the 8-digit number with 1.

3 To dial from one area from another in all other cases, preface the 8-digit number with 16.

The digits are read in pairs, thus:

31 56 67 09 Trente et un, cinquante-six, soixante-sept, zéro neuf.

## Verbs

| | | | |
|---|---|---|---|
| **être** *to be* | | **avoir** *to have* | |
| je suis | *I am* | j'ai | *I have* |
| tu es | *you are* | tu as | *you have* |
| il est | *he/it is* | il a | *he/it has* |
| elle est | *she/it is* | elle a | *she/it has* |
| nous sommes | *we are* | nous avons | *we have* |
| vous êtes | *you are* | vous avez | *you have* |
| ils sont | *they are (masc.)* | ils ont | *they have (masc.)* |
| elles sont | *they are (fem.)* | elles ont | *they have (fem.)* |

Verbs ending in:

| **-er** | **-ir** | **-re** |
|---|---|---|
| **travailler** *to work* | **finir** *to finish* | **vendre** *to sell* |
| je travaille | je finis | je vends |
| tu travailles | tu finis | tu vends |
| il travaille | il finit | il vend |
| elle travaille | elle finit | elle vend |
| nous travaillons | nous finissons | nous vendons |
| vous travaillez | vous finissez | vous vendez |
| ils travaillent | ils finissent | ils vendent |
| elles travaillent | elles finissent | elles vendent |

Verbs ending in **-er** generally, though not always, follow the pattern above. Verbs ending in **-ir** generally have the endings indicated above, but the form of the stem can change according to a variety of different patterns. Verbs with the basic form in **-re** are, unfortunately, very irregular.

We give some of the more common irregular verbs in the table opposite, but for full information you will need to refer to a dictionary or grammar book. (The **vous** form is not given separately, as it is usually formed by replacing the **-ons** of the **nous** form with **-ez**.)

For the sake of simplicity, the **tu** form of the verb – that is, the form for *you* used with family and close friends, – is also omitted in the table.

## A table of common verbs

|  | je | il/elle | nous | ils/elles |
|---|---|---|---|---|
| **acheter** *(to buy)* | achète | achète | achetons | achètent |
| **aller** *(to go)* | vais | va | allons | vont |
| **partir** *(to leave)* | pars | part | partons | partent |
| **venir** *(to come)* | viens | vient | venons | viennent |
| **recevoir** *(to receive)* | reçois | reçoit | recevons | reçoivent |
| **voir** *(to see)* | vois | voit | voyons | voient |
| **savoir** *(to know)* | sais | sait | savons | savent |
| **dire** *(to say)* | dis | dit | disons (vous dites) | disent |
| **écrire** (to write) | écris | écrit | écrivons | écrivent |
| **suivre** *(to follow)* | suis | suit | suivons | suivent |
| **comprendre** *(to understand)* | comprends | comprend | comprenons | comprennent |
| **lire** *(to read)* | lis | lit | lisons | lisent |
| **croire** *(to believe)* | crois | croit | croyons | croient |
| **boire** *(to drink)* | bois | boit | buvons | boivent |
| **connaître** *(to know, be acquainted with)* | connais | connaît | connaissons | connaissent |
| **faire** *(to do, make)* | fais | fait | faisons (vous faites) | font |

**vouloir** *to want to*

| | | | |
|---|---|---|---|
| je veux | *I want to, etc.* | je voudrais | *I would like to, etc.* |
| tu veux | | tu voudrais | |
| il veut | | il voudrait | |
| elle veut | | elle voudrait | |
| nous voulons | | nous voudrions | |
| vous voulez | | vous voudriez | |
| ils veulent | | ils voudraient | |
| elles veulent | | elles voudraient | |

**pouvoir** *to be able to*

| | | | |
|---|---|---|---|
| je peux | *I can, am able, etc.* | je pourrais | *I could, would* |
| tu peux | | tu pourrais | *be able to, etc.* |
| il peut | | il pourrait | |
| elle peut | | elle pourrait | |
| nous pouvons | | nous pourrions | |
| vous pouvez | | vous pourriez | |
| ils peuvent | | ils pourraient | |
| elles peuvent | | elles pourraient | |

See Units 1 and 2 for examples of how these two verbs are used.

## Adjectives

In Unit 4 we noted that in French many adjectives follow the noun they describe. It is also important to realize that, whether it comes before or after the adjective, the ending changes according to the gender and number of the noun. The usual pattern is as follows:

| **Masculine:** | le grand pull-over | *the large sweater* |
|---|---|---|
| | les grands pull-overs | *large sweaters* |

| **Feminine:** | la grande fenêtre | *the large window* |
|---|---|---|
| | les grandes fenêtres | *large windows* |

Other common patterns occur in the change from the masculine ending:
**-eau** to the feminine **-elle** (beau, belle: *beautiful*; nouveau, nouvelle: *new*),

and from the masculine:

**-eux** to feminine **-euse** (nombreux, nombreuse: *numerous*).
One very irregular one: vieux, vieille: *old*.

Don't let fear of making mistakes in this inhibit you from speaking
French! In most cases you will still be understood even if you
forget to make the adjective and noun agree. However it'll ease
communication if you learn the masculine and feminine forms of
at least a few of the commonly occurring adjectives.

# Vocabulary

## Notes

1 The gender of nouns is indicated by the article (**le**: masculine; **la**: feminine), except for those with the article **l'** or **les**; in these cases the gender is indicated by (m.) or (f.).

2 Feminine forms of adjectives are given in brackets.

3 The following abbreviations are used:

| | |
|---|---|
| abbr. = abbreviation | obj. = object |
| adj. = adjective | pl. = plural |
| f. = feminine | pron. = pronoun |
| m. = masculine | sing. = singular |
| n. = noun | subj. = subject |
| | tel. = telephone |

## French - English

### A

**à** at, in, to
**absent(e)** absent, away
d' **accord** O.K., agreed
l' **accueil** (m.) welcome
**accueillir** to welcome
l' **achat** (m.) purchase
le **service des achats** buying department
**acheter** to buy
**adapté(e) à** suitable, suited to
l' **addition** (f.) bill
l' **adresse** (f.) address
les **affaires** (f.) business
l' **âge** (m.) age
**âgé(e) (de cinq ans)** aged (five, five years old)
l' **agence** (f.) agency
**aider** to help
**aimer** to like, love
l' **Allemagne** (f.) Germany
**allemand(e)** German
**aller** to go
l' **allergie** (f.) allergy
**allô** hello (on tel.)
**alors** so, then

l' **an** (m.) year
l' **anglais** (m.) English (language)
l' **Angleterre** (f.) England
l' **année** (f.) year
**août** August
l' **apéritif** (m.) aperitif
l' **appareil** (m.) telephone
l' **appétit** (m.) appetite
**bon appétit!** enjoy your meal!
**apporter** to bring
**apprécier** to appreciate
**après** after
**après-demain** the day after tomorrow
l' **après-midi** (m. or f.) afternoon
**après-vente** after-sales
l' **artichaut** (m.) artichoke
l' **article** (m.) article
s' **asseoir** to sit down
**asseyez-vous!** sit down!
**assez** enough
l' **assiette** (f.) plate
l' **associé(e)** (m. or f.) colleague
**assorti(e)** matching
**attendre** to wait
l' **audit (interne)** (m.) (internal) auditor
l' **augmentation** (f.) increase

**augmenter** to increase
**aujourd'hui** today
**au revoir** good-bye
**aussi** also, too
**autre** other
**avant** before
**avec** with
**avril** April

## B

le **battant** shutter
**beau (belle)** beautiful, lovely
**beaucoup (de)** many, a lot (of)
la **beauté** beauty
le **beurre** butter
**bien** good, well
**bien cuit** well done (steak)
**bientôt** soon
la **bière** beer
**blanc (blanche)** white
**boire** to drink
le **bois** wood
**bon(ne)** good
**bonjour** good morning, good
  afternoon
le **bonnet** type of hat
la **bouteille** bottle
la **Bretagne** Brittany
**breton(ne)** Breton, from Brittany
la **brochure** brochure
le **bureau** office

## C

**ça** (abbr. of cela) that
**ça dépend** that depends
le **café** coffee
la **caisse** crate
le **calvados** calvados (type of liqueur
  made of apples)
le **camion** lorry
le **canard** duck
la **carte** (1) (business) card; (2)menu
le **carton** cardboard
le **cas** case
  **dans ce cas** in this case
**ce, cette, ces** this, that, these, those
**cela** that
**celtique** Celtic
**cent** hundred
le **centimètre** centimetre
**c'est** this is, it is

**c'est-à-dire** that is to say
**c'est à vous** it's your turn, it's up to
  you
la **chaîne de production** production line
**chaud(e)** hot
**cher (chère)** dear, expensive
**chercher** to look for
**chéri(e)** darling
**chez** at the home/workplace of, in
  the country of
le **chiffre** figure, number
le **chiffre d'affaires** turnover
le **chocolat** chocolate
**choisir** to choose
le **cigare** cigar
**cinq** five
le **citron** lemon
le **client** client, customer
le **cognac** cognac, brandy
le **colin** hake (type of fish)
le **colis** parcel
la **collaboration** collaboration
**combien (de)?** how much, how many?
la **commande** order
  **passer une commande** to place an
    order
  **sur commande** to order
**comme** like, as
**commencer** to begin
**comment?** how, what?
**comment allez-vous?** how are you?
la **communication** communication
  **en communication** on the line
**comprendre** to understand
la **comptabilité** accounting, accounts
la **concurrence** competition
la **condition** condition
les **conditions de paiement** terms of
  payment
la **conférence** conference, meeting
**confirmer** to confirm
**conforme à** compatible with
le **connaisseur** expert
**connaître** to know, get to know
**connue** known (see *connaître*)
**conseiller** to advise, recommend
le **constructeur** builder
**content(e) (de)** pleased (with)
le **contrat** contract
**convenir** to suit
  **ça vous convient?** does that suit you?
les **coordonnées** (m) details of self,
  company etc.
**coûter** to cost
le **crédit** credit

le **crédit documentaire irrévocable** irrevocable letter of credit
**croire** to think, believe
  **je crois** I think, believe (see *croire*)
la **croissance** growth
le **cuir** leather

## D

**dans** in, into
**de** of, from
**décafféiné(e)** decaffeinated
**décembre** December
**déjà** already
le **déjeuner** lunch
le **déjeuner d'affaires** business lunch
les **délais**(m) **de livraison** delivery times
**demain** tomorrow
**demi(e)** half
**dépasser** to exceed
en **déplacement** away on business
**depuis** for (a period of time), since (a point in time)
**déranger** to disturb
**dernier (dernière)** last
**désirer** to wish, want
**désolé(e)** sorry
le **dessert** dessert
**deux** two
  **tous les deux** both
le **devis** quotation
  **faire un devis** to give a quotation
le **diamètre** diameter
la **difficulté** difficulty
le **digestif** liqueur
**dimanche** Sunday
la **dimension** size
**dire** to say, tell
  **dites-moi** tell me (see *dire*)
le **directeur/la directrice** manager
**dix** ten
**à domicile** at home
**donner** to give
**sans doute** without doubt
**se douter de** to suspect
**je m'en doutais!** I thought as much!
**douze** twelve
la **droite** right
à **droite** on the right
**du** of the

## E

l' **eau** (f.) water
l' **échantillon** (m.) sample
**écossais(e)** Scottish
**écrire** to write
  **comment ça s'écrit?** how is that spelt?
**également** also, too
**élégant(e)** elegant
**elle** she, it
**elles** they (f.)
l' **emballage** (m.) packing
l' **employé(e)** (m. or f.) employee
**employer** to employ
**en** (1)in; (2)of it, of them
**enchanté(e)** pleased to meet you
**encore** still, yet
l' **enfant** (m.) child
**entendu** agreed
l' **entreprise** (f.) firm
**environ** about, approximately
l' **épaisseur** (m.) thickness
**épeler** to spell
l' **équipe** (f.) team
**est-ce que ...?** (indicates question)
**et** and
l' **été** (m.) summer
l' **étranger** (m.) abroad
**être** to be
  **elle est/il est** she is/he is (see *être*)
  **vous êtes** you are (see *être*)
**européen(ne)** European
**exactement** exactly
**excellent(e)** excellent
s' **excuser** to apologise
**exister** to exist
l' **export** (m.) exporting
  **le service export** export department
l' **extérieur** (m.) exterior
à **l'extérieur** outside

## F

**fabriquer** to manufacture
**facile** easy
la **facture** invoice
**faire** to do, make
  **ça fait** that makes, that comes to
  **ça fait partie de** that's part of
**fait à la main** hand-made
**familial(e)** family (adj.)
la **femme** woman, wife
la **fenêtre** window

**fermer** to close
**février** February
la **filiale** branch (of company)
la **fille** girl, daughter
le **foie gras** liver pâté
**fournir** to supply
le **fournisseur** supplier
**frais (fraîche)** fresh
la **fraise** strawberry
**français(e)** French
les **frites** (f.) chips
**froid(e)** cold
 **il fait froid** the weather's cold
le **fromage** cheese
le **fruit** fruit
les **fruits**(m.) **de mer** seafood
**fumer** to smoke

## G

la **gamme** range (of products)
**garanti(e)** guaranteed
le **garçon** (1) boy; (2) waiter
**gaseux (gaseuse)** fizzy
la **gauche** left
à **gauche** on the left
**gentil(le)** kind
la **glace** ice cream
**goûter** to taste
**grand(e)** big, large
**grave** serious

## H

**habiter** to live
l' **habitude** (f.) habit
 **comme d'habitude** as usual
**haut(e)** high, tall
l' **heure** (f.) **(1)** hour; (2) o'clock
**heureux (heureuse)** happy
l' **hiver** (m.) winter

## I

**ici** here
l' **idée** (f.) idea
**il** he, it
**ils** they (m.)
**il y a** there is, there are
l' **import** (m.) importing
 **le service import** import department
l' **indicatif** (m.) area code

**installer** to install
l' **instant** (m.) moment
l' **intention** (f.) intention
 **avoir l'intention de** to intend to
**intéressant(e)** interesting
l' **intérieur** (m.) interior
 **de l' intérieur** from inside
**interminable** interminable, endless
**inusable** hard-wearing

## J

**janvier** January
**je** I
**jeudi** Thursday
**jeune** young
**joindre** to reach, get hold of
**juillet** July
**juin** June
le **jus (de fruit)** (fruit) juice

## L

**la** (1) the (f.); (2) her, it
**là** there
**laisser** to leave (behind)
le **lait** milk
**large** wide
**le** (1) the (m.); (2) him, it
**léger (légère)** light (weight)
**les** the (pl.)
la **lettre** letter
la **ligne** line
la **liste** list
la **livre** pound (weight, sterling)
**livrer** to deliver
**long(ue)** long
la **longueur** length
**lui** to/for him/her
**lundi** Monday

## M

**ma** my
**madame** madam; Mrs
**mademoiselle** Miss
**mai** May
la **main** hand
**maintenant** now
**mais** but
la **maison** house; firm, company
**mal** bad(ly)

**pas (trop) mal** not (too) bad
**malade** ill
le **malentendu** misunderstanding
le **marché** market
le **marché intérieur** domestic market
**marcher** to work, function
**mardi** Tuesday
**marié(e)** married
le **marketing** marketing
 le **service marketing** marketing
 department
**mars** March
le **matin** morning
**me** (to) me
**même** same
le **menu** set menu
**merci (bien)** thank you (very much)
**mercredi** Wednesday
le **message** message
**mettre** to put
**midi** midday
**mieux** better
**mille** thousand
le **millimètre** millimetre
le **million** million
**minérale** mineral (adj.)
le **modèle** model, style
**moderne** modern
**moi** me
**moins** less
 **deux heures moins dix** ten to two
le **mois** month
le **moment** moment
le **monde** world
 **tout le monde** everybody
**monsieur** sir; Mr
**montrer** to show
le **motif** motif
**moyen(ne)** medium-sized, average

## N

**ne ... pas** not
**nettoyer** to clean
le **nom** name
**non** no
**normalement** normally
**normand(e)** Norman, from
 Normandy
la **norme** norm, standard
la **note** bill
**noter** to note
 **c'est noté** it's noted
**notre, nos** our
**nouveau (nouvelle)** new

**novembre** November
le **numéro** number
 **numéro de fax/ télécopie** fax number

## O

**occupé(e)** occupied, busy, engaged
**octobre** October
**offrir** to offer; give (a present)
**on** one, you
l' **orange** (f.) orange
**original(e)** original
**ou** or
**où** where
**oui** yes
l' **ouverture** (f.) opening
**ouvrir** to open

## P

le **paiement** payment
**par** per
 **par semaine** per week
**parce que** because
**pardon** pardon, excuse me
**parler** to speak
la **parole** word
la **part** share, proportion
 **quelle part de ...?** what share of ...?
 **de la part de qui?** On whose behalf?
 Who is it? Who's speaking?
la **partie** part
 **pas de problèmes** no problem
 **pas du tout** not at all
 **passer** to pass, hand over; go past; go
 on to
 **je vous le/la passe** I'm putting you
 through to him/her
 **patienter** to be patient, wait
le/la **patron(ne)** owner
le **P.D.G. (Président Directeur**
 **Général)** Managing Director
 **permettre** to allow
le **personnel** personnel, staff, workforce
 **petit(e)** little, small
un **peu** a little
un **petit peu** just a little, a little bit
 **peut-être** perhaps
la **pièce** part (e.g. of machine), spare
 part
le **plat** dish, course (of a meal)
 **pleuvoir** to rain
 **il pleut** it's raining
 **plus (de)** more (than)
 **plusieurs** several
la **poignée** handle

la **pomme** apple
**possible** possible
le **poste** extension (tel.)
**pour** for
**pourtant** nevertheless
**pouvoir** can, be able
  **je peux** I can (see *pouvoir*)
  **il/ elle pourrait** he/she could
**pratique** practical
**préférer** to prefer
**premier (première)** first
**prendre** to take
le **prénom** first name
**près de** near
à **présent** at the moment
**présenter** to present, introduce
la **pression** draught beer
**prier** to request
  **je vous prie** please
**principal(e)** main, principal
le **prix** price
le **problème** problem
**prochain(e)** next
la **production** production
  **le service de production** production department
le **produit** product
**proposer** to suggest
**propre** own
**puis** then
le **pull over** pullover, sweater

## Q

la **qualité** quality
**quand** when
**que** (1)that (e.g. I think that ...);
  (2)than
**quel(s), quelle(s)** which, what
la **question** question
**qui** who
**quitter** to leave (a place)
  **ne quittez pas** hold the line

## R

la **raison** reason
  **avoir raison** to be right
**rapide** quick
**rappeler** to call back
  **je rappellerai** I'll call back
le **rapport** relationship
  **par rapport à** in relation to

**regretter** to regret, be sorry
**remercier** to thank
la **remise** discount
le **rendez-vous** appointment
se **renseigner** to find out
**rentrer** to return
**répéter** to repeat
le/la **représentant(e)** representative
la **réunion** meeting
  **en réunion** in a meeting
**rien** nothing
  **de rien** don't mention it
**robuste** strong, robust
**rond(e)** round
**rouge** red

## S

**saignant** rare (of steak)
la **salade** salad
**samedi** Saturday
**sans** without
  **sans doute** without doubt
  **sans problème** no problem
la **sauce** sauce
**savoir** to know
  **je sais** I know(see *savoir*)
**sec (sèche)** dry
le/la **secrétaire** secretary
le/la **secrétaire de direction** the director's
  secretary
la **sécurité** security, safety
la **semaine** week
**septembre** September
**sérieux (sérieuse)** serious
le **service** (1) service (2) department
  **à votre service** at your service; (on
  tel.) speaking
la **serviette** briefcase
**seul(e)** alone
**seulement** only
**si** if
le **siège social** headquarters (of
  company)
  **s'il vous plaît** please
la **société** company, firm
le **soir** evening
la **soupe** soup
**spécial(e)** special
**spécialisé(e)** specialized
se **spécialiser** to specialize
le **steak** steak
le **stockage** stocking (of goods)
le **succès** success
le **sucre** sugar

**suivre** to follow
le **sujet** subject
au **sujet de** on the subject of, about
**sur** (1)on (2)by (dimensions)
**sûr(e)** sure, certain
  **bien sûr** of course

## T

la **taille** size
**tard** late
  **plus tard** later
la **tarte** tart
la **tartelette** small tart
**technique** technical
  **le service technique** technical
  services
le **téléphone** telephone
**téléphoner** to telephone
le **temps** (1)weather; (2)time
la **terrine** type of pâté
le **thé** tea
**tout, tous, toute(s)** all
  **tous les deux** both
  **tout à l'heure** soon
**traditionnel(le)** traditional
**transmettre** to transmit, pass on
**travailler** to work
le **travailleur** worker
**très** very
  **très bien** very good

**trop** too
**trouver** to find
**tu** you (used with family and friends)
**type** typical
**typique** typical

## U

**un, une** a(n); one
l' **unité** (f.) unit
l' **unité de production** production unit
**urgent(e)** urgent
l' **usine** (f.) factory
**utiliser** to use

## V

en **vacances** on holiday
**vendredi** Friday
la **vente** sale
  **le service des ventes** sales department
  **vers** at around (in time phrases)
**vos** your (with pl. noun)
**votre** your (with sing. noun)
**vouloir** to want, wish
  **je voudrais** I would like (see *vouloir*)
  **vous voulez** you want (see *vouloir*)
**vous** you
le **voyage d'affaires** business trip

## A

**a, an** un (une)
to **be able to** pouvoir
**about, approximately** environ
**about, on the subject of** au sujet de
**abroad** à l'étranger
**accounts dept.** la comptabilité
**address** l'adresse (f.)
to **advise** conseiller
**after** après
**afternoon** l'après-midi (m. or f.)
**after-sales service** le service
  après-vente
**agency** l'agence (f.)
**agreed** entendu, d'accord
**all** tout, tous, toute(s)
to **allow** permettre
**alone** seul(e)
**already** déjà
**also** aussi, également
**an** un (une)
**and** et
**aperitif** l'apéritif (m.)
to **apologize** s'excuser
**appointment** le rendez-vous
to **appreciate** apprécier
**approximately** environ
**April** avril
**area code** l'indicatif (m.)
**article** l'article (m.)
**as** comme
**at** à
**at around (time phrases)** vers
**auditor** l'audit (m.)
**August** août
**average** moyen(ne)
**away** absent(e)
**away on business** en déplacement

## B

**bad** mal
  **not (too) bad** pas (trop) mal
**beautiful** beau (belle)
**because** parce que
**beer** la bière
**before** avant

to **begin** commencer
to **believe** croire
**better** mieux
**big** grand(e)
**bill** l'addition (f.), la note
**both** tous les deux
**bottle** la bouteille
**boy** le garçon
**branch (of company)** la filiale
**brandy** le cognac
**Breton** breton(ne)
**briefcase** la serviette
to **bring** apporter
**Brittany** la Bretagne
**brochure** la brochure
**business (matters)** les affaires
**business trip** le voyage d'affaires
**busy** occupé(e)
**but** mais
**butter** le beurre
to **buy** acheter
**buying department** le service des
  achats
**by (dimensions)** sur

## C

to **call back** rappeler
**card** la carte
**cardboard** le carton
**case** le cas
  **in this case** dans ce cas
**centimetre** le centimètre
**certain** sûr(e)
**cheese** le fromage
**child** l'enfant (m.)
**chips** les frites (f.)
**chocolate** le chocolat
to **choose** choisir
**cigar** le cigare
**client** le client
to **close** fermer
**coffee** le café
**cold** froid(e)
**colleague** l'associé(e) (m. or f.)
**communication** la communication
**company** l'entreprise (f.), la société
**compatible with** conforme à

**competition** la concurrence
**condition** la condition
**conference** la conférence
to **confirm** confirmer
**contract** le contrat
to **cost** coûter
**course (of meal)** le plat;
  **of course** bien sûr
**credit** le crédit
**customer** le client

# D

**daughter** la fille
**day** le jour
  **the day after tomorrow** après-
  demain
**dear** cher (chère)
**decaffeinated** décaféiné(e)
**December** décembre
to **deliver** livrer
**delivery times (i.e. time taken to**
  **deliver)** les délais (m.) de livraison
**department** le service
**depend: that depends!** ça dépend!
**dessert** le dessert
**diameter** le diamètre
**difficulty** la difficulté
**director's secretary** le/la secrétaire de
  direction
**discount** la remise
**dish** le plat
to **do** faire
**domestic (market)** (le marché)
  intérieur
**doubt** le doute
  **without doubt** sans doute
to **drink** boire
**dry** sec (sèche)

# E

**easy** facile
to **employ** employer
**employee** l'employé(e) (m. or f.)
**engaged (on the tel.)** en communication
**England** l'Angleterre (f.)
**English** (adj.) anglais(e)
**English (the language)** l'anglais(m.)
**enjoy your meal!** bon appétit!
**enough** assez
**European** européen(ne)
**evening** le soir

**everybody** tout le monde
**exactly** exactement
to **exceed** dépasser
**excellent** excellent(e)
**excuse me** pardon
to **exist** exister
**expensive** cher (chère)
**expert** le connaisseur, l'expert (m.)
**export, exporting** l'export (m.)
**export department** le service export
**extension (tel.)** le poste
**exterior** l'extérieur (m.)

# F

**factory** l'usine (f.)
**family** (n.) la famille
**family** (adj.) familial(e)
**February** février
**figure** (numeral) le chiffre
to **find** trouver
to **find out** se renseigner
**firm** l'entreprise (f.), la société
**first** premier (première)
**first name** le prénom
**fish** le poisson
to **follow** suivre
**for (me)** pour (moi)
**for (a period of time starting**
  **in the past)** depuis
**French** français(e)
**Friday** vendredi
**from** de
**fruit** le fruit
to **function** marcher

# G

**German** allemand(e)
**Germany** l'Allemagne (f.)
to **get hold of (on tel.)** joindre
**girl** la fille
to **give** donner
to **give a quotation** faire un devis
to **go** aller
**good** bon(ne)
  **very good!** très bien!
**good-bye** au revoir
**good morning/afternoon** bonjour
**growth** la croissance
**guaranteed** garanti(e)

# H

**half**  demi(e)
**hand-made**  fait(e) à la main
**hard-wearing**  inusable
**he** il
**headquarters (of company)**  le siège
  social
**hello** (on tel.)  allô
to **help** aider
**her** (pron.)  la
**here** ici
**high**  haut(e)
**him** le
**hold the line!**  ne quittez pas!
**holidays**  les vacances
  **on holiday**  en vacances
**hot**  chaud(e)
**how?** comment?
**how are you?**  comment allez-vous?
**how much? how many?**  combien
  (de) ?
**hundred**  cent

# I

**I** je
**ice cream**  la glace
**idea**  l'idée (f.)
**if** si
**ill** malade
**import, importing**  l'import (m.)
**import department**  le service import
**in**  (1)en (France)  (2)à (Paris)
  (3)dans (cinq minutes)
to **increase** augmenter
**inside**  l'intérieur (m.)
to **install** installer
to **intend to**  avoir l' intention de
**interesting**  intéressant(e)
**interior**  l'intérieur (m.)
**into** dans
to **introduce** présenter
**invoice**  la facture
**irrevocable**  irrévocable
**it** (subj.)  il (m.), elle (f.)
**it** (obj.)  le (m.), la (f.)
**it is**  c'est

# J

**January**  janvier
**juice**  le jus (de fruit)

**July**  juillet
**June**  juin

# K

**kind**  gentil(le)
to **know (a person/place)**  connaître
to **know (facts)**  savoir

# L

**large**  grand(e)
**last**  dernier (dernière)
**late(r)**  (plus) tard
to **leave (behind)**  laisser
to **leave (a place)**  quitter
**left**  la gauche
  **on the left**  à gauche
**lemon**  le citron
**length**  le longueur
**less**  moins
**letter**  la lettre
**letter of credit**  le crédit
  documentaire
**light (weight)**  léger (légère)
**like**  comme
to **like** aimer
**liqueur**  la liqueur, le digestif
**list**  la liste
**little**  petit(e)
  **(just a) little**  un (petit) peu
to **live** habiter
**long**  long(ue)
to **look for** chercher
**lorry**  le camion
**(a) lot (of)**  beaucoup (de)
to **love** aimer
**lunch**  le déjeuner
  **business lunch**  déjeuner d'affaires

# M

**madam**  madame
**main**  principal(e)
to **make** faire
  **that makes ...**  ça fait ...
**manager**  le directeur/la directrice
**Managing Director**  le P.D.G.
  (Président Directeur Général)
to **manufacture** fabriquer
**many**  beaucoup (de)
**March**  mars

**market** le marché
**marketing** le marketing
**marketing department** le service
  marketing
**married** marié(e)
**matching** assorti(e)
**May** mai
**me** me, moi
**medium (of steak)** à point
**medium-sized** moyen(ne)
**meeting** la conférence, la réunion
  **in a meeting** en réunion
**mention: don't mention it!** de rien!
**menu** la carte
  **set menu** le menu
**message** le message
**midday** midi
**milk** le lait
**millimetre** le millimètre
**million** le million
**Miss** mademoiselle
**misunderstanding** le malentendu
**model** le modèle
**modern** moderne
**moment** l'instant (m.), le moment
  **at the moment** à présent
**Monday** lundi
**month** le mois
**more (than)** plus (de)
**morning** le matin
**Mr** monsieur
**Mrs** madame
**my** mon, ma, mes

## N

**name** le nom
**near** près de
**new** nouveau (nouvelle)
**next** prochain(e)
**no** non
**norm** la norme
**normally** normalement
**not** ne ... pas
**not at all** pas du tout
to **note** noter
  **it's noted** c'est noté
**nothing** rien
**November** novembre
**now** maintenant
**number, numeral** le chiffre
**number (house, tel., etc.)** le numéro

## O

**October** octobre
**of** de
to **offer** offrir
**office** le bureau
**O.K.** d'accord
**old (5 years old)** âgé(e) (de cinq ans)
**one (pron.)** on
**one (number)** un(e)
**only** seulement
to **open** ouvrir
**opening** l'ouverture (f.)
**or** ou
**order** la commande
**original** original(e)
**other** autre
**our** notre, nos
**outside** à l'extérieur
**owner** le patron, la patronne

## P

**packing** l'emballage (m.)
**parcel** le colis
**pardon** pardon
**part (of the whole)** la partie
  **(spare) part** la pièce
to **pass on (a message)** transmettre
to **be patient** patienter
**payment** le paiement
**per** par
**perhaps** peut-être
**personal details** les coordonnés
**personnel** le personnel
to **place an order** passer une commande
**plate** l'assiette (f.)
**please** s'il vous plaît, je vous prie
**pleased (with)** content(e) (de)
**pleased to meet you** enchanté(e)
**possible** possible
**pound (weight, sterling)** la livre
**practical** pratique
to **prefer** préférer
**price** le prix
**principal** principal(e)
**problem** le problème
  **no problem** pas de problème
**product** le produit
**production department** le service de
  production
**production line** la chaîne de production

**production unit** l'unité (f.) de production
**proportion** la part
**purchase** l'achat (m.)
to **put** mettre
**I'm putting you through** Je vous le/la passe

## Q

**quality** la qualité
**question** la question
**quick** rapide
**quotation** le devis

## R

to **rain** pleuvoir
**it's raining** il pleut
**range (of products)** la gamme
**rare (of steak)** saignant
**reason** la raison
to **recommend** conseiller
**red** rouge
to **regret** regretter
**relation: in relation to** par rapport à
to **repeat** répéter
**representative** le/la représentant(e)
to **return** rentrer
**right** à droite
**on the right** à droite
to **be right** avoir raison
**robust** robuste
**round** rond(e)

## S

**safety** la sécurité
**sale** la vente
**sales department** le service des ventes
**same** même
**sample** l'échantillon (m.)
**Saturday** samedi
to **say** dire
**seafood** les fruits de mer (m.)
**secretary** le/la secrétaire
**security** la sécurité
**September** septembre
**serious** grave, sérieux (sérieuse)
**service** le service
**at your service** à votre service
**several** plusieurs

**share** la part
**she** elle
to **show** montrer
**since (a point in time)** depuis
**sir** monsieur
to **sit down** s'asseoir
**sit down!** asseyez-vous!
**size** la dimension, la taille
**small** petit(e)
to **smoke** fumer
**soon** bientôt, tout à l'heure
to **be sorry** regretter
**(I'm) sorry** (je suis) désolé(e)
**soup** la soupe
to **speak** parler
**speaking (on tel.)** à votre service, à l'appareil
**who's speaking?** c'est de la part de qui?
**special** spécial(e)
to **specialize** se spécialiser
to **spell** écrire, épeler
**how is that spelt?** comment ça s'écrit?
**staff** le personnel
**standard** la norme
**steak** le steak
**still** encore
**stocking (of goods)** le stockage
**strong** robuste
**style** le modèle
**success** le succès
**sugar** le sucre
to **suggest** proposer
to **suit** convenir
**does that suit you?** cela vous convient?
**suited to** adapté(e) à
**summer** l'été (m.)
**Sunday** dimanche
**supplier** le fournisseur
to **supply** fournir
**sure** sûr(e)

## T

to **take** prendre
**tall** haut(e)
**tea** le thé
**team** l'équipe (f.)
**technical** technique
**technical services** le service technique
**telephone** le téléphone
to **telephone** téléphoner

to **tell** dire
**tell me** dites-moi
**terms of payment** les conditions de paiement
**than** que
to **thank** remercier
**thank you** merci, je vous remercie
**that (e.g. I think that ...)** que (je pense que ...)
**the** le, la, l', les
**then** (1)alors (at that time)
(2)puis (next, afterwards)
**there is, there are** il y a
**they** ils (m.), elles (f.)
**thickness** l'épaisseur (m.)
to **think** croire
**this, that, these, those** ce, cette, ces
**this is** c'est
**that** ça, cela
**thousand** mille
**Thursday** jeudi
**time** le temps
**what time is it?** quelle heure est-il?
**to** à
**today** aujourd'hui
**tomorrow** demain
**too, also** aussi, également
**too (much)** trop
**traditional** traditionel(le)
**Tuesday** mardi
**turnover** le chiffre d'affaires
**typical** type, typique

# U

to **understand** comprendre
**unit** l'unité (f.)
**urgent** urgent(e)
to **use** utiliser
**usual: as usual** comme d'habitude

# V

**very (good)** très (bien)

# W

to **wait** attendre, patienter
**waiter** le garçon
to **want** désirer, vouloir
**water** l'eau (f.)
**we** nous
**weather** le temps
**the weather's cold/hot** il fait froid/chaud
**Wednesday** mercredi
**week** la semaine
**welcome** l'accueil (m.)
to **welcome** accueillir
**well** bien
**well done (steak)** bien cuit
**what** quel(s), quelle(s)
**when** quand
**where** où
**which** quel(s), quelle(s)
**white** blanc (blanche)
**who** qui
**wide** large
**wife** la femme
**window** la fenêtre
**wine** le vin
**winter** l'hiver (m.)
to **wish for** désirer, vouloir
**with** avec
**without** sans
**woman** la femme
**wood** le bois
to **work** travailler
to **work, function** marcher
**worker** le travailleur
**workforce** le personnel
to **write** écrire

# Y

**year** l'an (m.), l'année (f.)
**yes** oui
**yet** encore
**you** tu (familiar); vous
**young** jeune
**your** votre, vos